From the Auth...
Five Steps to Acces...

AMY KEESEE
FREUDIGER

The
30
Day

HEALING
DARE

Dedication

I dedicate this book to my parents, Gary and Drenda Keesee, who have taught me to walk in the way of the Lord since I was young. I have learned so much from you. Thank you for being my parents, but just as importantly, thank you for being my pastors and teaching me how the Kingdom of God works. I love you both!

Table of Contents

THE DIFFERENCE OF 8 HOURS!

BEFORE AND AFTER:
13 POUNDS AND 9 INCHES GONE!

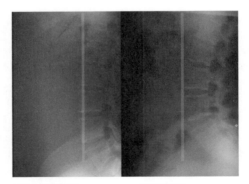

BEFORE
Spine is straight, intestines are displaced, mass in abdomen.

AFTER
Spine is curved, intestines are in place, mass is gone.

Introduction

I WAS HEALED OVERNIGHT, BUT THIS IS REALLY HOW IT STARTED.

I was a pastor's kid and a Christian who knew the Bible, but I was very sick.

I had seen many people healed, but when I started having health issues and the symptoms started adding up, fear gripped me.

It all started with pain and discomfort in my stomach and spine when I was around the age of 16. The symptoms started out mild, so at first I ignored them. But as they got worse and worse at age 19, I finally thought I should be checked out.

When the only symptoms present at that time were a hardness and protrusion of my abdomen, plus female issues, the doctor I first saw looked me over and said, "This is probably just the way you are." She had no way of comparing how I looked two years prior to how I looked then. She suggested that I was probably just insecure about my body, as many nineteen-year-olds are.

When my mom asked, "Shouldn't we get a CT scan?" the doctor said that it wasn't needed yet, but instead referred us to a hormone specialist. She thought I was so young that it was probably just a spinal shape imbalance or something I was imagining.

The next doctor found some irregularities in my hormone levels, so he started treating that but referred me to a different doctor for other symptoms. The next doctor prescribed me medication to deal with nausea and digestion issues, but again did not find or address the root cause.

Each doctor kind of brushed me off as very young and probably just paranoid. So what if I had a bit of a tummy? I should just eat health-ier, I was told. So I crash-dieted and lost some weight, but that only made my stomach look larger and the rest of my body appear smaller in comparison.

Fast forward several years, and I looked like I was five-to-six months pregnant! It was terribly embarrassing. But the spirits of rejection, self-hatred, and shame I struggled with were even worse than the pain. I couldn't even fight, because I felt so defeated and unworthy. I hated how I looked and felt. I was tormented.

I also started having severe nausea, infections in my organs, blood sugar swings, aches all over my body, female cycle irregularities, lack of curvature in my spine, acid reflux, hair loss, symptoms of nervous breakdowns, pain in my abdomen, and more. I couldn't stand the embarrassment, the not knowing how to fix it, the questions and bafflement of doctors....

After trying five doctors, I wanted off the medical merry-go-round, so I stopped going. They didn't seem to offer much except sugges-tions for treating the symptoms. They didn't know what these symp-toms were coming from, except to say my spine lacked curve and it could be muscular issues caused by that. That didn't explain the other stuff though.

Things only got worse.

Meanwhile, I met and married a wonderful guy named Jason, who knew my struggles but encouraged and loved me anyway. During our first year of marriage, I had multiple visits to emergency rooms and urgent cares. I was unable to go to work for at least 10 weeks out of that first year of marriage either because I felt so terrible or because of serious infections in my organs that cropped up out of nowhere.

Often, I wouldn't tell Jason just how bad I felt, simply saying I had decided to work from home that day so as not to see the concerned look on his face. I would cry as soon as he left for work each time, because I felt frightened and alone in my struggle.

Much of that was my own decision not to let anyone in on how I felt. I knew Jason and my parents would want to take me to another doctor, who would again have no answers.

In an effort to deal with the muscular and spinal pain, I had gone to a kinesiologist, therapeutic masseuse, and a chiropractor. The first day at the chiropractor, he took an X-ray and showed me that there was indeed a mass in my abdomen and my organs were displaced, much like a pregnant lady's. His recommendation was to go and see a specialist, but he also said, "It's nothing that God can't handle."

I knew I had a choice. I could either continue to stay on the medical merry-go-round or I could find out WHY I had not been able to receive my healing.

I knew God COULD heal, but I just couldn't seem to believe that *I* could be healed. In fact, for years, I had "tried" to "get healed."

I had many people pray for me. It didn't work.

I had begged God to heal me. It didn't work.

I had gone to plenty of doctors. It didn't work. I had tried quoting Scriptures for a day or two. It didn't work.

Something was wrong.

I just couldn't understand why healing wasn't "working" for me—for *nine* miserable years.

Until one day.

That was the day I had a massive cry fest, and I got alone in my prayer closet to have a "come to Jesus meeting." I asked the Lord to please show me what I was missing and told Him that if He would show me what to do, I would do it—whatever it was.

I told Him, "Lord, I want to be a mommy. I want to have kids. Whatever it takes, I want this issue taken care of THIS YEAR. I'm done with being sick!"

That was the moment when the Holy Spirit challenged me to what I call my "30-day Healing Dare." He told me to do certain things for 30 days, and I said YES!

During those 30 days, God revealed five key principles that totally changed my outlook on life. In this devotional, I focus on and break down these five principles.

- Days 1 through 9 focus on the principle of reclaiming your identity and discovering who you are in Christ Jesus.
- Days 10 through 17 illuminate how to repaint your picture

of possibility, building your faith in order to receive.

- Days 18 through 24 show you how to stand in the authority and strength God has given you, even in the midst of any storm.
- Days 25 through 27 talk about praying the prayer of faith and making contact with the healing power of Jesus.
- And finally, days 28 through 30 share the principle of praising God for the victory, even when you may not see it happen immediately.

You'll also find encouraging stories of victory scattered throughout.

Why 30 Days?

One of the greatest things God showed me when I was begging for healing was that I was living in *hope*, not *faith*. The remedy? He specifically told me to take 30 days to renew my mind and take hold of absolute trust in His Word. A 30-day Dare would be enough time to:

- Detox from the negative messages and thoughts that had been holding me back.
- Discover who He said I was.
- Invade my mind and body with Truth from the Word of God.
- Repaint my picture of possibilities so that I could see myself healthy and healed.
- Build my faith to the point that God looked bigger than my problem.

- Overcome the hopelessness and sadness that had overtaken me.
- Defeat self-hatred and shame once and for all.

When I finally understood the five principles, which I will share in this book, and once I walked through the 30-day Healing Dare, my heart drastically changed.

Then, one morning two weeks after the 30-day Healing Dare ended, I woke up completely healed overnight!

I had lost 13 pounds and 9 inches in my waist overnight as I slept! My spine was curved. No more pain, no more infections. No more nausea. No more aches. I had a brand-new body! I had a brand-new freedom to match it!

I was instantly and dramatically healed and have been walking in freedom from sickness for more than 10 years now.

Since then, I have been sharing my story, and we have seen many people healed as a result. I am extremely passionate about getting the good news out to those who are suffering, because I've been there. It's not fun. It's not God's best for our lives.

If you haven't read my testimony book, *Healed Overnight: Five Steps to Accessing Supernatural Healing*, I would encourage you to get a copy. In *Healed Overnight: Five Steps to Accessing Supernatural Healing*, I tell my story in more detail, give you the five keys to healing that God showed me during my journey, answer common misconceptions and lies about healing, and more!

Friend, God wants to do a miracle in your life… and, in fact, He wants miracles to be an everyday occurrence! A miracle is defined as something that defies earthly laws but should be NORMAL in our lives because we answer to a higher law—the law of life!

Big Things Will Happen in the Next 30 Days

Give God the opportunity to renew your faith during the next 30 days, commit to the 30-day Healing Dare just like I did, and watch what happens.

Put this devotional into practice and I promise you that your faith will soar and your joy will skyrocket. Friend, nothing can hold you back when your faith grabs hold of God's promises. It changes everything!

Tools

YOUR DAILY FAITH BOOSTERS

To really receive all of the benefits of this study, you will need to do a few things.

These steps are not a formula for healing, but rather, faith boosters to build your faith muscle quickly.

Do these daily:

1. **Read the day's devotion and answer the questions at the end, using a separate journal.** Each day's devotion will expand on one of the five keys God taught me and will end with a Scripture to look up and read, a daily "detox," a self-reflection, the day's takeaway, and a prayer.

   I know it's easy to move on to the next thing in your day, but I encourage you to really stop and ask the Holy Spirit what He is speaking to you each day. Look up the Scriptures at the end of each devotion and SAY them as you read or write them. Let the Truth sink in. Think about the devotion and the Scriptures for the rest of the day. Meditate on them continually.

2. **Say NO to negativity!** Do everything you can to turn off the negative messages coming through movies, music, social media, news, people, doctors, or even your own mouth. Make a conscious decision to keep your mind on good things. Delete the apps. Turn off the TV. Create positive playlists of music and great healing teachings to boost your results.

Finally, brothers and sisters, whatever is true, whatever is noble, whatever is right, whatever is pure, whatever is lovely, whatever is admirable—if anything is excellent or praiseworthy—think about such things.

—Philippians 4:8

3. **Speak the Word!** Using the healing Scriptures in the appendix, SPEAK the Word OUT LOUD *at least three times per day.* (Yes, out loud!) You need to hear yourself speaking the Word often. The Word is your healing medicine! Put your favorite healing Scriptures on paper, on your lock screen, in your bathroom—everyplace where you will see them throughout the day.

4. **Write your own confession of faith and speak it daily.** This is your declaration of what you are receiving from God. If you're not sure what I'm talking about, I will go over it in detail in one of the upcoming day's devotions. My confession that I spoke daily is in the appendix at the end of this book, for your reference.

5. **Worship like it's your weapon.** Whenever you get a chance, put on anointed worship music that focuses your attention on Jesus and His might. Get alone, stand to your feet, raise your hands, or bow before the Lord. Get your whole self involved until you feel a breakthrough. This daily practice will help you fight fear and receive the amazing presence of the Great Physician, Jesus.

6. **Take care of your temple.** Ask God if there are practical ways

to promote healing in your life. God's wisdom for our bodies can include a better diet, at least 30 minutes of movement per day, adequate sleep at night, drinking enough water, etc. It can include starting to take supplements, with the recommendation of a doctor or naturopath.

One pastor we know who was diagnosed with colon cancer felt led to go on a raw veggie diet and to drink a large amount of barley grass in liquid every day. He is healed and whole today.

The point is, do your best to take care of the amazing gift of your body. Some people suffer because of the way they abuse their bodies. One guy we know was drinking hundreds of milligrams of caffeine per day when it finally resulted in a complete breakdown of his adrenal glands and massive panic attacks. As soon as he detoxed from the caffeine, the symptoms left.

Enjoy the Journey

Your journey through this 30-day Healing Dare will be exciting, encouraging, and eye-opening! I pray it paints a confident picture of hope for you and for anyone who needs healing.

My prayer is that you continue to pull out this 30-day Healing Dare anytime you need to move a mountain in your life, whether it's illness, financial hardship, a broken heart, a lack of confidence, a loss of dreams—anything. Whatever you need, it requires faith in God, and these 30 days are all about building, nourishing, and protecting faith. You can receive all the promises of God through faith in Him, as you will see throughout this devotional. The same principles apply to every area and need of your life. Jesus has made a way for you to live in a place where the earth curse (sin, death, sickness, poverty) has NO EFFECT on you! It's a new realm, a totally different dimension that is free from cares, fear, pain, or lack. It's the Kingdom realm, a supernatural place to walk through life with victory, no matter the attack against you!

Whatever the attack that has come against your future, Jesus said that you have the power to speak to it and see it stop. You can speak to the mountain and watch it move. I didn't say that; God, Himself did.

It's hard to argue with God. When He says it's possible, He means it's possible.

Remember, I am no more special to God than you are! What He did for me, He has promised in His Word to do for ALL who believe! But there are keys to unlocking these great and precious promises.

Vision

YOUR PERSONAL FAITH GOALS

NOTE:

I encourage you to keep a personal journal during your 30-day Healing Dare. It can be any sort of plain journal or notebook—or you can get my *Healed Overnight Scripture Journal*. Any time you see the journal icon throughout this devotional, grab that and answer the prompts, starting with the section below. Even if you aren't a big writer, just keeping a record of your journey is a step of faith, a way to mark the mile you are walking toward your future. Those who take the time to do this daily reap significant results!

Let's take a moment before we start this Dare to get a clear picture of what we are aiming toward. Please think about and answer the following questions.

What do you want to see change in **yourself** at the end of your 30-day Healing Dare?

What is the one **circumstance** you want to see change at the end of your 30-day Healing Dare?

Many people experience a disconnect between God's promises and their realities, between what God says about life and how they are experiencing life.

What are some of those disconnects in your life? *List them one by one, and be specific. (Avoid emotions and try to pinpoint what is **causing** those emotions. For example, instead of listing "discouragement," put "discouraged because I feel like I've been coping with pain for so long.")*

Vision Board Challenge: People say that a picture is worth a thousand words, but did you know a picture also silences a thousand doubts? Every time your brain sees an image, it believes in it just a bit more. It builds a neural pathway of belief in your brain! When you see a photo of something, it silences the question about whether that thing exists or is possible. So I want you to take a moment, using the goal you set above, to create a vision board that includes the following:

- Find a few photos, images, drawings, and words that exemplify or show exactly what your goal(s) will look like when fulfilled. What could you do? How would you feel? What could you eat/wear/accomplish when you are completely healed, pain free, etc? For me, I had a photo of a cute swimsuit I wanted to wear after my abdomen didn't look huge. I had photos of me prior to getting sick. I had photos of places I wanted to travel to and physical activities I wanted to do once healed.

One of my friends, who was extremely sick and bedridden, took a pair of sparkly high-heeled shoes into a major surgery, because she wanted to hold on to the picture of her wearing those again. She had those by her bed at all times to remind herself that she would one day wear high heels and keep marching forward toward her mission.

Another lady, a mother with a very crippled and sick little girl, placed a beautiful lace dress next to her daughter so she could see it. That crippled little girl imagined herself wearing that dress after Jesus healed her.

In both of these examples, these individuals experienced supernatural healings.

- Now, place those items in a prominent place where you will see them every day. You can put them on a bulletin board, wall, mirror, or piece of presentation board. Just make sure it's somewhere that you cannot miss on a daily basis. (I have an entire vision wall in my bedroom that is filled with images of what we are believing God to do, see, or accomplish!)

- As you go about your day, make sure to stop and look at those images, and then thank God for them!

Vision will propel you and keep you from quitting. If you're not sure what your vision should be, beyond deliverance from the problems you're facing, or you don't know why God placed you on this earth, let's look at some hints about your calling and purpose:

1. Your most important job description and main reason for still being here on Earth is called "The Great Commission" (Matthew 28:16-20). It says to go into all the world and preach the Good News, making disciples. The vocation or *way* in which you fulfill that is just the vehicle to carry the Gospel to others. Those in your realm of influence need to hear and see you living out the Gospel, preaching the Good News with words and actions, whether that's to your kids, grandkids, neighbors, or coworkers. You being healed is key to your ability to carry out this Great Commission with longevity and effectiveness.

2. What knowledge, experience, or wisdom have you acquired that you can share with others? Someone needs you! Someone needs your testimony. Someone needs to see Jesus through you.

3. What is the dream in your heart that just won't die? Maybe it's been there all your life, and you've said, "One of these days...." Friend, don't wait till one of these days if it's something that can help someone today. God placed that dream inside of you!

4. What are the things God has spoken over your life through words of prophecy or confirmations to you in the Bible? His calling on your life does not go away. The vision might take a while, but wait for it. He who promised is faithful.

All right, are you ready to dive into day one of your 30-day Healing Dare? I want you to GET YOUR FAITH UP and get excited, because BIG things are going to happen when you grab hold of a God who is more than enough!

"Isn't it a comfort to know that we worship a God who cannot be exaggerated?"

~Francis Chan

THE 30-DAY HEALING DARE

FROM SURGERY TO CELEBRATION

DAY 01

Welcome to day one of your 30-day Healing Dare!!! Are you ready to break out of the pain, negativity, and fear that have held you back? I know that God's Word WORKS, and as you put in the work to meditate and speak it, the power and anointing that is on those words will transform you—spirit, soul, and body.

It might not happen instantly, and that's okay. You might not feel anything in your emotions at first, but it will happen. Your body might not react immediately, but be assured, God's words are not average or spoken lightly. When He speaks, He means it!

I told my story briefly in the introduction. (Time to backtrack, you Introduction skipper! Haha!) Now I want to share the story of someone else who took a 30-day Healing Dare, with amazing results! Her name is Rikki, and several years ago, my friend Liz gave her a copy of my testimony book, *Healed Overnight: Five Steps to Accessing Supernatural Healing.*

For many years, Rikki had suffered from severe fibroid tumors. She had already had one procedure to shrink them, but they came back—this time even larger. Her doctor told her, "It is impossible for these to go away on their own."

The tumors were causing all manner of pain, symptoms, and embarrassment, as her abdomen noticeably protruded. She couldn't exercise. She was constantly uncomfortable. In fact, she had many of the same symptoms I used to have, which is why our mutual friend gave her my book.

She had multiple tumors, and two of them were the size of baseballs, so her doctor scheduled her for a hysterectomy. She was out of breath all the time because the tumors were pressing on her organs and lungs. She said it felt similar to being pregnant.

Then Rikki received my book. She wrote on the title page: "Today, I scheduled my surgery for 9 Aug... BUT GOD." As she started reading my book, she said she felt offended at first. She wondered why God had healed me but had not healed her. Back to Rikki's story in a second...

You Have a Choice

When people like me claim that Jesus wants to heal *everyone*, it can offend some people. After all, it seems radical to this fallen world's state of sickness and death. And every time you try to believe God for something like healing, satan is immediately going to try and convince you otherwise. He doesn't want you healed or prosperous or changing other people's lives! He wants you broke, sick, fearful, angry, and depressed.

That's where you have a choice: Who are you going to listen to? Are you going to listen to satan or those he uses to tout his messages of fear and death? Or are you going to run to God's message and listen to what He has to say about you and your life? Now, let me finish telling you Rikki's story.

Rikki made the decision to keep reading my book, and when she saw where I shared that she, too, could be healed, she got excited! She felt led to do what I did and take her own 30-day Healing Dare because she did NOT want to have the hysterectomy surgery.

Rikki later told me, "I got serious about this because I wanted it. I saw where you had written in your book that Jesus never told anyone 'no' when they asked Him for healing. I thought, *Then he won't tell me no!*" She told me, "Surgery isn't a bad thing, but I knew it wasn't a *Rikki* thing."

Rikki put her faith fully in the Great Physician, Jesus, who already paid the price for her healing. With just weeks until her scheduled surgery, she made a quality decision to take what was already hers—HEALING. Her faith grabbed hold of the promises of God concerning her physical body!

She was so convinced of Jesus's healing promise to her and so convinced she would not need surgery that she scheduled herself, her daughter, and her mother to complete a 5K run happening the weekend after her scheduled surgery date! Her faith said she would run a 5K instead of getting surgery, even though she hadn't been able to run at all due to the tumors. She didn't sit around moping and hoping. Instead, she took action and scheduled that 5K run. She knew, according to the Word of God, it was already done in the spiritual realm, because:

Faith sees the "after" picture when you are still living in the "before."

One morning, less than halfway through her 30-day Healing Dare, Rikki woke up, got ready for work, and stepped out the door. Then the Holy Spirit stopped her. He told her to go back to bed. It didn't make sense, but she was obedient. When she lay down, the Holy Spirit said, "Now touch your stomach." As she touched her stomach, she realized *the fibroid tumors were gone!*

Jumping up and looking in the mirror, she saw the reality of what her faith had already seen in the spirit. She was completely healed! Those two hard masses had simply disappeared. She was no longer short of breath! She felt great!

She called her doctor, ecstatic to tell him the good news, but his office refused to schedule a checkup. He told her over the phone, "It's impossible for those to go away on their own. We will see you at your pre-operation appointment the day before surgery."

Rikki hung up the phone in shock. They wouldn't even listen to her!

Fine, she thought. *I'll just wait and show the doctor that God easily does impossible things!*

Rikki went to her pre-op appointment and insisted they do another ultrasound. The nurse rolled her eyes and went to get the doctor. When he finally came in, he looked annoyed but then stunned when he saw her stomach.

He did the ultrasound, then checked and checked again. *He could not find anything!* Flustered and irritated, he blurted out, "I'll see you in six months to make sure they haven't come back," as he huffed out of the room. Rikki immediately started praising God, telling the nurse that Jesus had healed her.

The surgery was cancelled!

That day, I received a text from my friend Liz concerning Rikki. When I read it, my jaw hit the floor and tears rolled down my cheeks.

Amy, my coworker Rikki just got the confirmation from her doctor—she no longer needs surgery!!!

I couldn't stop the tears of joy, because I know all too well what it's like to go from having no hope to being healed, from living with pain for years to being in total health in a moment, from coping with a broken body to suddenly walking whole.

I remember like it was yesterday the morning that I awoke to a pain-free, tumor-free body. The joy is indescribable! And it all starts the moment faith grabs hold of the promise, before it manifests in the natural realm.

Rikki, her daughter, and her mother ran the 5K together that weekend, and Rikki says she laughed the whole way.

God IS real. God IS able. God IS willing. God IS here. He is ready to do the same for you!

Receive it, much like a confident child receives a gift from their parent.

Don't be offended when you hear of someone else's victory. Instead, say, "If God did that for them, He will do it for me too!"

Friend, it's time for you to receive this wonderful gift of healing. It's time to put your doubts to rest and become convinced that it is indeed God's desire to heal you.

DON'T FORGET!

As you finish today's devotion, don't forget to flip to the healing Scriptures in the appendix and read them out loud several times today.

 **READ**

Mark 5:21-42

 DETOX:

Have you been "moping and hoping" while feeding on a constant stream of doubtful thoughts? Write down three doubtful thoughts that jumped into your brain as you read Rikki's story or when you tried to think about your own body being healed. Where do you think those doubts came from?

1.

2.

3.

 SELF-REFLECTION:

Now, do as the Bible says and "take captive every thought," making it obedient to God (2 Corinthians 10:5)!

Say, "Fear and doubt, get out! I will not live in unbelief any longer! Instead, I choose to believe. I serve the God of the impossible!"

Picture yourself grabbing those negative thoughts, putting handcuffs on them, and throwing them in jail!

TODAY'S TAKEAWAY:

I will focus on what's possible instead of the negative messages of the enemy.

PRAYER

Jesus, help me to commit to doing whatever it takes during these 30 days to receive all the good things You have given me. I dedicate this month to You, and I ask You to walk with me. Speak to me. Lead me. Hold me. And, as the disciples prayed, help my unbelief.

RECLAIM YOUR IDENTITY

JUST THE WAY YOU ARE

DAY 02

"That's just the way you are," said the doctor as she looked at my body.

"You're going to have to learn to cope with it," said another doctor.

Everywhere I turned, I was told that there was something wrong with ME. Meanwhile, there was an inner voice, that had been there since childhood, telling me I wasn't as good or as pretty or as loved as others. I was stuck with "me." "You are the problem," the devil whispered.

The first section of this 30-day Healing Dare is dedicated to our first step in receiving healing, and that is:

1. Reclaim your identity. (Find out who God says you are.)

We must focus on building healthy identities so we know who we are in Christ Jesus. Why? Because:

- Physical health is first an identity issue.
- Unless you know who you are, you will never have what belongs to you.
- Healing is yours because of who you are—God's kid.
- You will not feel good until you believe that you *are* good.
- You must be able to picture yourself having the good things God wants to shower on you—and if you can't, it's time to repair some broken places in your heart.

Most people believe God is good, but they don't see themselves as good enough. I know I didn't. You see, the devil had convinced me that I was seriously lacking in lots of ways. I fell into the comparison trap constantly. I had a serious, raging identity crisis going on in my mind and heart at the time. I didn't feel worthy enough to be heard, to be loved, or even to relax. I couldn't seem to stop worrying about other people's opinions of me. I couldn't see myself walking in and fulfilling the dreams I had for my life.

I couldn't look in the mirror without feeling crushed. What I saw was not the pretty, fresh-faced dreamer that I was. That beautiful girl was buried beneath layers of pain and shame until I could no longer see her. I see photos of myself from my early twenties, and it makes me so sad to remember how I mistreated myself. I only saw "ugly." The only thing I liked about myself was my eyes.

I would cry just trying to get dressed, going through outfit after out-fit in an attempt to not only cover my protruding stomach but also to cover my inner rejection.

Have you ever been there? I was really good at acting happy and content in front of people while being miserable and treating myself terribly in private. More than anything, I was terrified of being exposed or vulnerable about how I felt. I was ashamed that I felt ashamed, if that makes sense! Shame brought more shame and caused me to hide. I didn't want people to know something was wrong with me. It took years for me to realize that a demonic stronghold of self-hatred had taken up residence in my mind and that I had to surrender all of that pain to God in order to be free.

The beginning of freedom happened one day as I stood in front of a mirror and told myself, "I hate my body. I just wish it would go away." Inside, I felt the Holy Spirit *YELL*:

"STOP IT! STOP HATING WHAT I LOVE! YOUR NAME IS BELOVED! SO LET YOURSELF BE LOVED!"

It took my breath away, because I realized I couldn't look at myself and say I was beautiful. I realized how much it hurt God when I called His creation ugly. I knew this condemnation and rejection weren't from God, but I didn't know how to be free. I fell to my knees, cried, and begged the Holy Spirit to help me.

He prompted me to schedule an appointment with a lady elder in our church. I didn't tell her what was wrong, but as we sat there, she started speaking by the Holy Spirit. She called out the generational root of rejection. She said words I had only spoken to God. She affirmed my worth, my value, my identity, and my calling. It was medicine to my soul! At the same time, my mind tried to reject each word of affirmation that she spoke over me. But the Holy Spirit inside of me was shouting, *"YES! That's what I've been trying to tell you!"*

That day, I set out on a journey to walk in total freedom from those roots of rejection. Through a week-long fast from food, and through the clarity it brought to my soul, I continued to hear the peaceful, quiet voice of the Holy Spirit.

He instructed me to find a Scripture to combat each lie I had believed about my identity and to write each of those Scriptures on 3x5 cards and place them all around my room. As I began speaking these Scriptures daily, I felt the rejection slowly lose its grip. I could stand in front of a mirror and say, "I love my body. I am beautiful."

It took months, but slowly, I felt my self-worth and value begin to rise. The questions that plagued me constantly—questions like, *"Will I ever be good enough?"*—started to be replaced with affirmations from the Word of God.

Amazingly, once the filter of rejection through which I saw the world was removed, my relationships and responsibilities got so much easier. Life took on a brand-new feeling. It was the feeling of BELONGING! I belonged to Jesus, and He belonged to me. What sweetness! What safety! No more striving! No more worrying! No more comparing myself to others!

I stopped believing that first doctor's words, that "this was just the way I was" and started believing God's words. I learned that "the way I was" looked totally different to God than it did to me. I saw *broken*, but He saw *beautiful*. I saw *lacking*, but He saw *lovely*. I saw *rejected*, but He saw *redeemed*.

And that's what He sees in you too.

You delight God's heart because He is your Father. He doesn't make junk! He doesn't leave one person deficient in the skills and giftings they need for life yet give another person what it takes.

God doesn't create anything that isn't absolutely, stunningly reflective of Him.

We look like our Daddy God! And I think you can agree He is perfect.

Let's continue this discussion tomorrow. To finish out today's devotion, let's take some time to reflect and meditate.

 **READ**

Write out 1 John 3:1 and speak it out loud as a personal affirmation, putting your name into it:

DETOX:

Write down three beliefs about your identity that have held you back from living life with freedom:

1.

2.

3.

SELF-REFLECTION:

What do you really think of yourself? Here's a good indicator: Can you sit alone, close your eyes, and think about yourself without having negative thoughts or pictures?

Ask the Holy Spirit to speak to your heart about what *He* thinks about you. Write down anything you hear or feel in your journal.

TODAY'S TAKEAWAY:

I was created in God's image, and He doesn't make junk.

PRAYER

Jesus, help me to receive what You say about me and who you say I am instead of what others have said or what I have said about myself. Help me feel valuable, loved, worthy, and free from shame.

RECLAIM YOUR IDENTITY
THE WAY BACK HOME

Once there was a young man who left home, and took his inheritance early despite his father still being alive. Oh, how it broke his father's heart when his son left home! The son went on a wild spree, squandered the inheritance with lustful living, and took on a completely different identity in order to gain friends and influence. He no longer lived as his father's son. Instead, he lived for himself, as a rebel without a cause.

Finally, he ran out of money. To make matters worse, the country he had moved to also became plagued with a severe famine. The only way he kept from starving was by working at a farm feeding pigs and eating whatever they left behind.

With no dignity left, one day he came to his senses. He thought about who he was and from where he had come. He was, after all, the son of a wealthy man, who provided for many servants. He thought, *Even my father's servants live much better than I do right now.* He longed to be back in his father's embrace, but he also knew that he had hurt and shamed his father with his behavior. Still, he decided to go home and beg for mercy, offering himself up as a servant, because he believed he no longer deserved to be called "son."

One morning, the father looked out over the horizon and saw a figure in the distance. As it came into focus, he recognized the gait, the stature, then the face. But could this ragged, gaunt, filthy man be his son? It was!

In that moment, the father forgot that he was a wealthy landowner with a dignified presence in the city, one who should not be seen running in the hot sun to embrace a vagabond. All that mattered was that he was a father desperately seeking his lost son. What must his son have gone through to look so dreadful?! Emotion choked his voice as he grabbed his son in a bear hug.

Not wanting anyone to see his beloved son in such a shameful state, covered in pigs' mess, he removed his own royal robe and wrapped it around the young man.

But he didn't stop there. He wanted to make a point to all who saw his son that all was forgiven and that he was still an heir of the estate. So he took off his signet ring and put it on his son's finger. And he took off his own shoes and put them on his son's blistered, scorched feet.

And then he threw a party! His lost son had returned!

For the son, his identity as a son was restored.

Jesus told this parable in Luke 15:11-24 as a parallel to another story—one that He came to play a major role in.

At the beginning of the year that I started my Healing Dare, this story was illuminated in my spirit. I somehow identified with the lost son, even though I had been a Christian from a young age. I saw his shame, and I recognized it in myself.

I realized I had some deep-seated beliefs about myself that needed healed. God showed me that the roots of the illness I battled were actually shame and fear, which resulted in sickness, unworthiness, rejection, and self-hatred. A broken spirit had resulted in a broken body (Proverbs 17:22). He also showed me that shame and fear are part of the curse that came upon mankind when Adam and Eve left their created identities and stepped into sin.

The Earth Curse, the Beginning of Identity Issues

At the beginning of time, God wanted a family, so He created children who had intellect, imagination, creative force, capability, and free will to choose Him as their One True Love.

Adam and Eve (the first created humans, God's first children) were fashioned by God's own hand and given His breath of life. They and all their descendants would be God's children, the apple of His eye, the ones His heart loved. Genesis 2:25 says, "*Adam and his wife were both naked, and they felt no shame.*" They had never known sin, shame, death, fear, pain, or lack. They only knew perfect acceptance, breathtaking love, and complete protection.

Can you imagine? They were like little kids—totally innocent and joyful! They knew who they were and to whom they belonged.

Adam and Eve were given positions of authority, to rule over the earth. (See Genesis 1:28). Hebrews 2:6-8 (TPT, emphasis mine) puts it this way:

> But the Scriptures affirm: What is man that you would even think about him, or care about Adam's race. You made him lower than the angels for a little while. *You placed your glory and honor upon his head as a crown.* And you have given him dominion over the works of your hands, for you have *placed everything under his authority.*

Smack dab in the middle of the Garden of Eden was a tree called "The Tree of the Knowledge of Good and Evil." God told Adam and Eve that if they ate of its fruit, they would surely die.

Why did God put the tree there if He knew it would tempt them? Because He had to.

Because satan was already on Earth when man was created, God had to give Adam and Eve a choice. It was in the act of choosing His will over satan's that they received His power. As long as they aligned themselves with God, they had authority over satan. They were given rulership—authority—over everything on Earth AS LONG AS THEY OBEYED GOD. (For more on this important principle, please read my dad, Gary Keesee's, book *Your Financial Revolution: The Power of Allegiance.*)

The devil was already on the earth, and he wanted the position of authority God had given Adam and Eve. The only way for him to take that would be to get these humans to align with him instead of with God, so he started lying to them about their identities.

The devil kept tempting Adam and Eve to taste the fruit that was forbidden. He told them they would be like God if they did, knowing good and evil. (The fact was, they were *already* like God, made in His image. And they already knew good; they just didn't know evil.) Satan made Eve feel as if she was missing something, implying that she wasn't enough.

And Adam and Eve fell for it. They chose to disobey; and in doing so, they left their Father. They aligned themselves with the devil's will instead of God's will.

When Adam and Eve chose to "leave their Father's house" and follow the voice of the deceiver, they lost their created identities and positions of authority, essentially handing it over to their new master. They also lost the inheritance that came with their Father's last name.

And immediately, their spirits went dark. They fell from their glorious identities. Even though they didn't physically die immediately, their spirits died—they became separated from God. They fell under a curse, the earth curse. And immediately, shame and fear became their lifelong companions.

Now they truly were lacking and broken. Their identity as God's perfect children was dashed on the rocks of sin, resulting in shame. Their first reaction once they had sinned was to hide. Suddenly, they knew what evil was.

Soon after, God called to them in the Garden of Eden, to spend time with them as He always did. But He could not see them because their spirits had gone dark. The saddest verse in the Bible, in my opinion, is Genesis 3:9 (NKJV). It says, *"Then the Lord God called to Adam and said to him, 'Where are you?'"* In those few words, I hear the heartbreak of a parent losing their child. I hear a father searching for H
is son and daughter. I've lost my child in the grocery store for a few minutes, and the sickening panic that struck me cannot compare to what God must have felt knowing what was about to happen.

Adam finally showed his face and said to Father God, *"I heard you in the garden, and I was afraid because I was naked; so I hid"* (Genesis 3:10, NIV). Adam had never felt fear until then. He had never known he was naked until then. He and Eve were frightened by their own Father, the One they had never hidden from before.

Now, as a result of their rebellion against their Father, all of their children's children would be born under the earth's curse. All of humanity—us included—lost our identity as rulers under our heavenly Father's leadership. We lost our places of authority and our inheritance as God's heirs. The human race plunged into spiritual darkness, translated into a lost realm filled with chaos, questions, and lack of purpose.

It has been said that evil is the absence of good, and that's what Adam and Eve experienced that day. They were separated from Love, Himself. Adam, from whom all of us were born, had made the choice to touch the tree and eat its fruit. He abandoned his created identity. He aligned himself with the will of another master. He left his Father's house, just like the Prodigal Son did. And he forfeited his birthright in the process. He lost his right to health and provision, peace and security.

The Fall was a departure from perfect identity in God into shame and fear, just like the Prodigal Son departed from his father's house and then thought he could no longer be called "son." As a result, we are all born with this problem: We don't remember who we are. We are separated from our Father's house. We are lost, starving for love, eating whatever scraps the world throws our way, and longing for acceptance. We are born in a land of famine—a dog-eat-dog, every-man-for-himself, survival-mentality world. We have it ingrained into our brains.

Along with the fall of man came other consequences. Painful toil would be required for survival. Thorns and weeds would choke out the food sources. Women would suffer in childbirth. Longing for love and acceptance would become a constant driving force. And all living creatures would degenerate physically. Sickness, decay, death, and suffering were used by the devil as a way to break the backs of God's beloved children. Satan hated Adam and Eve and all of their descendants, because they were created in God's image.

Searching for Something

Mankind has been searching for their identities ever since. To this day, satan tries to convince us that we are worthless in order to keep our eyes veiled to the true identity bestowed on us at creation. Thus, deep inside of every person, there is still a longing for the feeling of home, all while living in a world stricken with a "famine of purpose." Every single person on this earth walks around with an invisible sign on them that says, "Make me feel special. Remind me who I am."

People give away their virginity in relationships to feel accepted. They join sports teams or gangs or clubs or sororities in order to feel like they belong. People seek pleasure and possessions to numb the pain of loneliness and longing. They cover their nakedness with social masks to hide their empty souls. As C.S. Lewis said in his book *Mere Christianity*,

> *If I find in myself desires which nothing in this world can satisfy, the only logical explanation is that I was made for another world.*

Our hearts long to walk in God's presence with all our needs met, as Adam did in the Garden of Eden. We were created for love and belonging, with every need supplied and every fear abolished in our Father's protective arms. In every human heart, there is a longing for Eden.

But God Made a Way

Thankfully, a search party was sent. A way back home was made so that we could find our identities as God's children once again. A New Covenant was established with all who call on Jesus. He came into the world to show us once again who we really are. He came to restore our royalty, authority, and true spiritual lineage.

Jesus told the story of the Prodigal Son to illustrate this story of rebellion, separation, redemption, and restoration. He showed us how badly <u>Father God wants to restore our identities, authority, and inheritance</u>.

The entire Bible is an epic saga of a Father seeking His children, a love story of longing to restore what once was. That's why Jesus came—to show us the way back home. He showed us our Father's heart. He came to remind us of the Kingdom where we belong. He came to restore our identities. Because of Him, we don't have to remain in a lost state, wandering aimlessly without a home. Jesus came to redeem and ransom us out of the kingdom (jurisdiction) of darkness back into God's family, the Kingdom of Life and Love. He came to restore everything that Adam lost in Genesis 1-2!

When we believe in the Lord Jesus Christ and receive the declaration of victory that He signed with His own blood, we inherit a restoration of our identities as children of our Father. We receive the full rights and benefits of being a child of God once again, just as Adam and Eve had in the Garden. In fact, we are now coheirs with Christ (Romans 8:17). We have been adopted back into His arms (Ephesians 1:5). He is our hiding place and a safe refuge from the storms of life (Psalm 91). He wants us to walk in a place of contentment and fellowship as His beloved (Ephesians 1:4-6).

Jesus set us free from the curse that came at the Fall. Galatians 3:13-14 (NKJV) say,

> *Christ has redeemed us from the curse of the law, having become a curse for us (for it is written, "Cursed is everyone who hangs on a tree"), that the blessing of Abraham might come upon the Gentiles in Christ Jesus, that we might receive the promise of the Spirit through faith.*

Jesus made a way of escape from anything that came as a result of the Fall, which brought the earth under a curse. That includes freeing us from pain and sickness. Just like the Father of the lost son restored the son's title and inheritance, Jesus restored to us the whole estate so that we can walk in a place of peace and security. We are wrapped in His robes of righteousness to cover our shame. We have His signet ring of authority, which gives us power over all the powers of the devil (Luke 10:19). Father God embraces us as His children, with no thought of our previous sins. I don't know about you, but that makes me want to celebrate! Isaiah 61:7 describes it like this:

> *Instead of your shame you will receive a double portion, and instead of disgrace you will rejoice in your inheritance. And so*

you will inherit a double portion in your land, and everlasting joy will be yours.

The Prodigal Son from Jesus's parable thought he had to become a servant because of the shame he had brought on himself. However, his father accepted him with no questions asked—and Jesus does the same for us.

He doesn't require us to pay our way back into His arms, because He paid it all.

He doesn't require us to earn the title of child, because He freely restored our identities.

He doesn't ask us to do penance for our sins, because He took the penalty for us.

He, Himself is our restoration. He covered our shame with His perfect righteousness. He gave us His authority. He restored our inheritance, including the blessing of Abraham. Talk about humbling! I absolutely love this Scripture, and I want to challenge you to meditate on it today:

> *Now we're no longer living like slaves under the law, but we enjoy being God's very own sons and daughters! And because we're his, we can access everything our Father has—for we are heirs because of what God has done!*
> —Galatians 4:7 (TPT)

READ

Look at Galatians 4:7 and then write it out, putting it in first person. Say it out loud a few times.

DETOX:

Take this quick survey to determine if you are living out of a place of victory in our Father's house or out of a place of survival in the realm of this earth curse system. Circle what best applies to you. (*Hint:* You can identify the answer to these questions by thinking about your prominent thoughts and beliefs when faced with circumstances day to day.)

	Victory *You Know Your True Identity*	**Survival** *You Need Your True Identity Restored*
My thoughts tell me I am:	in a place of more than enough and that God provides.	in a place of famine like the Prodigal Son, and I must fight to survive.
I have been:	enjoying loving fellowship and deep relationship with my Father God.	walking in slavery, fear, and shame, and God feels distant.
I often think thoughts about myself that make me feel like I am:	deeply loved, fully chosen, and accepted by God, because I know I'm His.	not good enough, or I'll never be able to fulfill my dreams. I am hard on myself.
I most often:	dream about winning in life and am not afraid of the future.	worry about surviving and deal with anxiety when I wonder about the future.
I most often:	make decisions based on my trust in God.	make decisions based on fear and insecurity and feel I must protect myself.
I most often:	believe that I can make progress and change.	battle thoughts that things will never change or that I am powerless.

SELF-REFLECTION:

The Prodigal Son had a wrong perception of his identity, so he took his life into his own hands and went out on his own. He left the protection and provision of his father's house. Are there things in your life now that, just like the Prodigal Son, you are trying to solve in your own strength, outside of your Father's house? If so, what are they?

 # TODAY'S TAKEAWAY:

Jesus made a way for me to be a part of the household of Father God, well cared for as His dearly-loved child.

PRAYER

Jesus, show me who I am as your child, and speak to my heart about how I can receive Your love for me. I receive back my identity, my authority, and my inheritance through the price You paid for me. Amen!

RECLAIM YOUR IDENTITY

A RESTORATION OF ALL THINGS

DAY 04

I was in Italy with my husband having dinner at a tiny local *ristorante* housed in a stone cottage. After enjoying the absolutely amazing Italian meal, we walked out of the ristorante and got into our rental car. Suddenly, a pounding on the door of the car startled us. I looked up to see our waiter, who barely spoke English, frantically waving my purse at the window. I gasped! I didn't even realize I had left it. We were two hours from our hotel, with several stops still to go, and I could have gone through the rest of the day without realizing that my purse, with all of my money and identification required to fly home, was sitting at that table.

Luckily, the waiter was kind enough to race to the rescue. I rolled down the window, gratefully received my purse back, and thanked him profusely. He was more than happy to help, and walked away with a smile on his kind face. Whew, that was a close one!

Without my passport identifying me as a U.S. citizen, and without my money allowing me to obtain all that I needed on my journey, I would've been in huge trouble. Until that waiter rushed out, I had no proof of my citizenship or rights, and no provision.

Our journey through this life is much the same. Many of us have misplaced our identities. But the Holy Spirit is there to remind us of what we have lost.

Your Inheritance

If we are Christians, with citizenship in our Father's house, we are part of God's Kingdom. If we call Jesus our Lord and Savior, we have been given His entire "estate" as our inheritance. We have a restoration of all things lost in the Garden of Eden. We thus have spiritual access to the health and provision given to us in God's will, the Bible. However, many have lost sight of this, causing them to misplace their identities and citizenship. They live like they are lost and destitute, sick and impoverished, just like those who are not Christians. They act like there's no hope. Pastor Craig Groeschel calls this being a "Christian atheist" and defines it as "people who believe in God but live as if He doesn't exist."

With the salvation that Jesus gave us came a restoration of belonging AND a restoration of rights. He handed us the keys to the Kingdom and said, "Here ya go, my child! It's all yours!" (See Matthew 16:19.) So why aren't we all living in that Truth, without fear or lack? Perhaps it's because we entered through the door of our Father's house but stopped there. Let me explain.

Another way to look at our inheritance as children of God is to imagine that when we were born again, our Father gave us the keys to a fabulous estate. The mansion on this estate is filled with luxurious, well-appointed rooms, breathtaking vistas, and wonderful aromas. Imagine that each of these rooms represents a different promise of God, such as peace, healing, rest, provision, joy, purpose, freedom, etc. Got the picture?

Now, let me ask you, have you entered the mansion but stopped in the foyer? Maybe you've opened the door and entered into the Father's house using the key that Jesus gave you (salvation), but is that where you've stopped? Sure, you're saved, but have you checked out all of the rooms filled with everything you need for life? There's a key for every room in the house! Have you seen how amazing the Banquet Hall of Healing is, laden with a delicious feast of health?

After all, Jesus called healing "the children's bread" (Matthew 15:26). Have you opened the door to the Parlor of Peace and sat down to rest? (See Psalm 23.) Have you enjoyed the answers that are in the Library of Wisdom or taken a dip in the Pool of Forgiveness? These are just metaphors, of course, for what God has provided, but God's promises are indeed real. He has given us the keys to all of these rooms within His estate.

Perhaps you have simply stood in the foyer—hungry and tired but not taking the steps forward to enter these wonderful places, all of which you can freely access.

Friend, GET OUT OF THE FOYER!

Come on inside and enjoy the richness and extravagance of God's love for you! Sit down and make yourself at home, for He has invited you in and seated you at His table. His banner over you is love (Song of Solomon 2:4). Explore what's yours. Read God's will, left to you in the Bible, and then take steps into the house. Go past salvation, albeit the greatest gift of them all, and start acting like a child of the estate. Receive ALL that God has given you.

Your Kingdom inheritance includes healing. <u>You have a citizen's RIGHT to walk in health.</u> I know that's a big statement, one that maybe you've never heard or understood. I'm going to explain and break down that statement throughout the rest of the book, but trust me when I say I've lived in pain and I've lived in health. Health is better. I lived in the foyer, and then I opened the door and entered the room called "Healing." It's a beautiful place. So let's get you out of the foyer....

Welcome to Healing

Bread is something that we eat to sustain our bodies in the physical world. It's an everyday staple that people the world over enjoy. As I mentioned, Jesus called healing "the children's bread" in Matthew 15:26. In other words, it is a normal, everyday thing to which we all have access. As my dad says, we have a right to say, "Pass the biscuits!" because we are invited to be seated at Father God's Banquet Hall of Healing. He has prepared a feast before us in the presence of our enemies, in the valley of the shadow of death, so that we don't have to fear! What's at our Father's family dinner table? Healing. Provision. Love. Answers. Rest. Forgiveness. Strength. David said it like this:

> *You prepare a table before me in the presence of my enemies. You anoint my head with oil; my cup overflows. Surely your goodness and love will follow me all the days of my life, and I will dwell in the house of the Lord forever.*
>
> —Psalm 23:5-6

Sure, we are surrounded by a land of famine, just like the Prodigal Son in the parable we read in the last devotion. But our Father provides for us as His dearly beloved children. We are living in a world that is saturated with fear, sickness, death, questions, and searching, because this earth is still under a curse. However, we don't have to live like those with no hope. We have a way of escape through the Kingdom of God. In Luke 12:31-32, Jesus said:

> *But seek his kingdom, and these things will be given to you as well. Do not be afraid, little flock, for your Father has been pleased to give you the kingdom.*

In this Kingdom, healing is part of what has been provided for us, because death itself was defeated. All sickness is a form of death in the body, but Jesus set us free from the curse of death:

> *For sin's meager wages is death, but God's lavish gift is life eternal, found in your union with our Lord Jesus, the Anointed One.*
> —Romans 6:23 (TPT)

The penalty for all sin is death, which originally entered the picture as a result of Adam and Eve's sin. Health is simply freedom from all forms of physical death. Through Jesus, we have been given access to life, including life in our spirits, souls, and bodies:

> *He himself bore our sins in his body on the cross, so that we might die to sins and live for righteousness; <u>by his wounds you have been healed</u>.*
> —1 Peter 2:24 (NKJV)

You Have the Whole Estate

Children are heirs to what their parents have. When a parent writes a will, they leave to their children what they possess in terms of wealth, resources, real estate, businesses, etc. In the same way, God has made us heirs to His "estate," giving us what He possesses. God doesn't have sickness; He has health. He doesn't have poverty; He has plenty. He doesn't possess fear; He possesses love, joy, and peace. He willed all of that to us!

If you have what God has, you have health. It comes as part of your identity as His child. In other words, "healed" is not what you are *trying to become*; healed is **who you are**!

It is part of your restored identity and inheritance as a child of God. Since 1 Peter 2:24 says that you HAVE BEEN healed, then you ARE healed. Say that: *"I AM healed."* All "I Am" statements are affirming your identity. (When you say, "I am ugly," or "I am a failure," you are actually making statements about your identity.) So when the Bible says you WERE healed, you can confidently proclaim, "I AM healed!"

What Adam lost in terms of the Garden of Eden and living as God's child, Jesus returned to us and more. Jesus became the doorway through which we enter into all of God's blessings. In other words, Jesus is the access point to becoming God's child once again. He came to the earth to pay off our debt of sin and buy us back out of slavery, setting us free. He is the only road to heaven. He is the Savior through which we obtain forgiveness and mercy. When He was crucified on the cross, freely giving Himself as a sacrifice for our sin, He cleared the path home. John 14:6 says, *"Jesus answered, 'I am the way and the truth and the life. No one comes to the Father except through me.'"*

John 10:9 (NKJV) says, *"I am the door. If anyone enters by Me, he will be saved, and will go in and out and find pasture."* That word "pasture" makes me picture a beautiful, lush, green meadow filled with contented sheep at perfect peace knowing that the shepherd is watching over them. Psalm 23:1-3a (NIV) say,

> *The Lord is my shepherd, I lack nothing. He makes me lie down in green pastures, He leads me beside quiet waters, He refreshes my soul.*

Thanks to God, we have a pathway to restoration of all that was lost in the Garden of Eden. We can live in a place of having all our needs met. We can walk with God in fellowship, as friends and confidants. We can walk in full authority and confidence.

Your Covenant

Back in the time before Jesus came, the Jewish people of Israel had a covenant with God, written about in Deuteronomy 28.

A covenant is a firm oath between two parties that says, "If you will _____, I will _____." God gave the children of Israel a long list of blessings that are summed up by Deuteronomy 28:6 (NLT), *"Wherever you go and whatever you do, you will be blessed."*

But that covenant included a long list of dos and don'ts—*laws*— that the people had to follow in order to obtain righteousness. It was their "I will" to God's "I will."

Throughout the Old Testament before Jesus, we see the children of Israel NOT holding up their end of the bargain, and thus they often didn't experience the blessing of the Old Covenant. The Law, including the Ten Commandments, was there to show them what was right and wrong, but their sin nature made it difficult for them to live perfectly. So Jesus came to give us a New Covenant. It's one that does not require us to be perfect, because Jesus was perfect, and He gave us His perfection. Hebrews 8:6-8 (TPT) say:

> *But now Jesus the Messiah has accepted a priestly ministry which far surpasses theirs, since he is the catalyst of a <u>better covenant</u>*

which contains far more wonderful promises! For if that first covenant had been faultless no one would have needed a second one to replace it. But God revealed the defect and limitation of the first when he said to his people,

> *"Look! The day will come, declares the Lord, when I will satisfy the people of Israel and Judah by giving them a New Covenant."*

We have a New Covenant that's even better than the old one. So what is God's "I will" in this agreement? The very first sermon Jesus ever preached listed the things He would do, and here's the list, paraphrased from Isaiah 61:

- Give good news to the poor. (The good news is that the poor can have all they need, according to His riches and glory.)
- Give freedom to the captives. (We are freed from anything that holds us back.)
- Release prisoners from darkness. (We are freed from anything that darkens our spirits or our vision/sight, because Jesus is our light.)
- Give God's favor to us. (*Favor* means *friendly regard, approval, obliging acts freely granted, acts of kindness given.* God blesses us with kindness.)
- Comfort those who mourn. (Comfort comes from removing whatever is causing pain, which is exactly what Jesus did when He bore our sorrows on the cross.)
- Provide for those who grieve. (Grief comes when something is lost. Jesus says He will provide. In other words, instead of loss, there will be provision.)

- Crown us with beauty for our ashes. (Ashes are the leftovers from destruction. Jesus brings order and beauty back, rebuilding what was destroyed.)

- Give us joy instead of mourning. (Notice that mourning is mentioned twice. *Mourning* means *the act of sorrowing*. Painful toil and sorrow came in the curse of the Fall. Jesus came to remove sorrow and replace it with joy.)

- Break off the spirit of despair, causing us to wear praise instead. (We can praise God because despair is no longer a part of our destinies.)

- Strengthen us to be like oak trees, displaying His power. (We are no longer weak, helpless, or hopeless. We should display God's splendor and strength.)

- Bless us through strangers and foreigners who don't even know us. (The wealth of the wicked is laid up for the righteous, according to Proverbs 13:22)

- Make us priests and ministers of God. (We can step into a place of ministry to others and take up our rightful places of authority in our Father's house.)

- Provide us with the wealth of nations. (Much like the wealth of Abraham, David, and Solomon caused foreign dignitaries to marvel, our lives will attract the favor of nations.)

- Give us a double portion of blessing instead of shame. (Shame says we aren't enough, but Jesus came to give us MORE than enough!)

- Give us an inheritance that causes us to rejoice in place of our former disgrace. (Disgrace like the Prodigal Son experienced is replaced with the inheritance of the Kingdom of God.)

- Give us everlasting joy. (We have a forever home in heaven, and our names are written in the Lamb's Book of Life. That is the everlasting joy of our salvation.)

- Array us in robes of righteousness. (Just as the Prodigal Son was wrapped in his Father's robes, God dresses us in His royal right standing.)
- Clothe us in salvation. (He washes us clean and claims us as His own with His saving power.)
- Cause righteousness to spring up in us. (As we learn about the Kingdom of God, we learn more and more about what God calls good and right. That starts to bear fruit, springing up in every area of our lives.)

Wow! That all sounds like really good stuff, right? That's God's "I will" in this New Covenant! Incredible.

Our Part

So what's our "I will" in this New Covenant? It's pretty simple. Since this New Covenant is not something we must earn or become good enough to obtain, it's something we obtain by faith. We must:

- <u>Believe</u> on the Lord Jesus to receive salvation (Acts 16:31).
- <u>Love</u> the Lord our God with all our hearts, minds, souls, and strength and love our neighbors (others) as we love ourselves (Luke 10:27).
- <u>Seek first</u> the Kingdom of God and His righteousness (what He calls right), and ALL THESE THINGS will be added to us. (By "all these things," Jesus is referring to everything we tend to worry about in life; see Matthew 6:25-33.)

So if sorrow and pain, grief and despair have been broken off of me, as a child of God living in His restoration of all things, I don't have to allow sickness to dwell in my body. I can walk in my identity and call sickness out as an illegal trespasser. I can demand that it leave because it is on Father God's property. I can tell pain that God's New Covenant set me free.

If I am walking in my fully created and restored identity, I will not permit anything in my life that God would not permit in the Garden of Eden. I will not just live in the foyer of this newly inherited estate, but I will walk into all that He has provided for in the New Covenant. I won't allow the deceiver, satan to talk me out of who I am and what I have been given as God's child!

That doesn't mean you or I won't encounter temptations or voices calling us away from His perfect will, but it does mean that we can resist them when we know who we are and Whose we are.

If only Adam and Eve would have stopped listening to the deceiver, who was calling them away from God's will. If only you and I would simply turn and say, "Shut up, devil! You're a liar!" whenever we hear the words of shame or fear or condemnation.

When we are holding our Father's hand, the world doesn't tempt us, the darkness doesn't scare us, and the devil can't touch us. We know the Shepherd is leading us, and we are perfectly content to just be His children. He has led us back home.

 **READ**

Look up 1 Peter 2:9, write it out, and meditate on it. Then speak it out loud, making it a first person "I Am" statement.

Write out Romans 8:15-16 and meditate on them. Then speak them out loud, making it a first person "I Am" statement.

 **DETOX:**

What crutches have you been leaning on in order to prop up a false identity in your life? Is it a high-powered career, keeping up appearances, spending too much money, keeping important friends, running to food as comfort, etc.? Look for things that you run to when you are feeling bad about yourself instead of running to God. List those things in your journal.

SELF-REFLECTION:

What areas of your life need the power of the New Covenant to change them? In what areas are you still "living in the foyer?"

 # TODAY'S TAKEAWAY:

I have a covenant with God, and healing is provided in that. I have access to healing because He gave me the keys to His entire estate. That's my inheritance as a coheir with Christ.

PRAYER

Father God, I come to You right now and ask You to restore my identity and how I see myself. Help me to fully know and understand who I am in Christ and what I have in the New Covenant. Call me back home to that place of total trust and peace in Your arms.

RECLAIM YOUR IDENTITY

DIGGING UP THE ROCKS

DAY 05

One day, I was praying with someone who was battling a chronic illness, listening for what I should pray. Suddenly, I felt the Holy Spirit ask gently, *"Is there sin in their heart against a leader?"*

That surprised me, and I felt uncomfortable asking, but I was obedient. This person confessed, with tears in their eyes, that they had indeed left their former church offended with that pastor and had also spoken against him to others. This person knew it was an issue that needed to be dealt with. They committed to me that they would go back and apologize to all who had been affected, including that pastor.

I knew this would be pivotal to their healing, not from a "God-is-punishing-you" perspective but from a "shut-the-door-on-the-devil" perspective. It was for their own freedom that they needed to forgive and ask for forgiveness. That unforgiveness and gossip were poisoning their heart and causing ongoing emotional pain. Sickness was simply a symptom of that.

Healing starts from the inside out. Third John 2 (TPT) says, *"Beloved friend, I pray that you are prospering in every way and that you continually enjoy good health, just as your soul is prospering."* The condition of the heart is what God is most concerned about. Why? Because all of the issues of life flow out of it (Proverbs 4:23).

The Rocks in Your Garden

During my own 30-day Healing Dare, God spoke to me about some rocks that were in my life. I had hardened my heart through unforgiveness, pride, and failure to release hurts. Those things had to go if

I wanted to be free. He had me write letters of forgiveness, call people I had hurt, and release pain from past rejection. Those things were hurting my heart.

- Gossip
- Offense
- Pride
- Stubbornness
- Unforgiveness or hatred
- Anger at God
- Unresolved bitterness or rebellion toward authority figures
- Willful sin

These are all what I call "rocks," and they cause a heart to become hard. They affect WHO we are as much as WHAT we can receive from God.

These rocks block God's Word from taking root and can cause our lives to become difficult places for good things to grow. They poison our souls, and as a result, hurt our bodies.

Jesus talked about the rocks and illustrated that they block blessings:

> *Then he told them many things in parables, saying: "A farmer went out to sow his seed. As he was scattering the seed, some fell along the path, and the birds came and ate it up.* **_Some fell on rocky places, where it did not have much soil. It sprang up quickly, because the soil was shallow. But when the sun came up, the plants were scorched, and they withered because they had no root._** *Other seed fell among thorns, which*

grew up and choked the plants. Still other seed fell on good soil,
where it produced a crop—a hundred, sixty or thirty times what
was sown. Whoever has ears, let them hear.

—Matthew 13:3-9

So what does this parable mean? The soil represents the heart because it's the place from which everything in our lives grows. My dad calls the heart "the incubator" (and yes, you'll notice how many things I've learned from my dad and mom in this book!) It will either produce a crop of good, nourishing plants or an infestation of stubborn, inedible weeds. If someone has a hard heart, the seeds of the Word of God will be rejected or "scorched." Hard hearts are closed hearts. Hard hearts are uninhabitable hearts. Hard hearts block healing.

Rocks in a person's heart stack up, and build a wall that resists God and forms a barrier against other relationships to the point that deep mistrust, isolation, and loneliness result. They also block out the voices of authority figures so that we can't hear the Truth.

No good thing can grow in darkness or isolation. It takes the light of God to grow good things. Unfortunately, as Jesus warned, some of us allow the Word of God to die before it ever takes root, because we haven't tended to our garden soil (hearts).

A man came up to me one day after I shared my story at a church, and with tears in his eyes, he said, "I really want to believe what you just taught on healing, but I can't."

I responded, "I'm sorry to hear that, but may I ask why?"

With a sudden bitterness in his tone, he said, "I'm really trying, you understand. But my mom died of cancer after praying and begging God to heal her. She was a good person. She had lots of other people praying for her. But she still died. I guess I'm mad at God. I don't understand how He could do this."

At that point, I felt deep compassion for him, because I, too, had at one time shut out the Truth due to a hard heart. I also understood that it was critical for him to dig out the rocks of bitterness and hurt that had taken root. God was his only hope, but he had built a wall that was keeping God's love and Truth out. He was blaming God for the grief of losing his mother.

Listen, it is life or death that you understand this: *God only does good* (John 10:10). He is your answer, not your problem. This young man seemed to believe that God was the problem because He had not intervened for his mom. But Jesus DID intervene for his mom when on the cross 2,000 years ago, He paid for a New Covenant with His blood and cried out, "It is finished!" (Remember from the last chapter that Jesus established a New Covenant for mankind when He died and rose again.)

I explained to this young man that God does not cause or allow sickness, but instead He has given us the "keys to the Kingdom" to receive healing through faith. I will share more about the nature of our Father at a later time, but know that it is crucial that you dig up any bitterness or disappointment you have toward God and realize that it was planted there by satan to separate you from Him!

Like in that young man's situation, a heart can become hard after it gets hurt, by people or by situations, and often people blame God for bad things that happen. Hurts or offenses become rocks if they remain unsurrendered to God. It's almost like "scar tissue" in the body after you get an injury. If that scar tissue is not softened or removed, it becomes immovable, painful, and tough. In the same way, offenses that are allowed to build up in the heart cause it to become immovable, arthritic, diseased, and barren. We tell ourselves that we are just trying to protect ourselves from being hurt again by harboring these offenses or unforgiveness. But in reality, we are hurting ourselves worse than we are hurting anyone else.

Jesus taught the urgency of forgiveness when He said:

> *Therefore, if you are offering your gift at the altar and there remember that your brother or sister has something against you, leave your gift there in front of the altar. First go and be reconciled to them; then come and offer your gift.*
> —Matthew 5:23-24

In other words, if you're worshipping in church and remember there is an offense between you and someone else, go immediately to make it right. Words of apology and forgiveness are a great way to keep your heart soft before the Lord. It's not a suggestion; it's a necessity.

Other times, our hearts are hardened because we turn our backs on God's warnings about sin, which is born out of pride in our lives. Pride can make us feel justified or okay to break the laws of God against ourselves or against someone else. And then, if we habitually say yes to sin and stop listening to the Holy Spirit, our hearts become calloused to His voice. We can't hear Him any longer because we've built a wall. We have shut Him out.

For the record, when God asks us to stay away from something and calls it "sin," it's not to keep us from having a good time. It's because He is trying to save us from hurtful, destructive consequences. If I tell my child, "Stop! Don't put that poison in your mouth!" it's not because I'm being mean. I'm actually being a loving parent by saying no. In the same way, God knows that sin will harm our lives. For instance, when God says not to go sleeping around and to save intimacy for marriage, He is trying to protect our hearts from abuse and pain.

Softening the Soil

So how do we dig up the rocks and soften the soil of our hearts? How do we change the hostile environment that rejects the Truth?

It starts with repentance. It is only out of humility that the Holy Spirit can be invited in to do His healing work. Only He can soften a hard heart.

King David, who had just seriously sinned and reaped a whole lot of bad fruit due to it, prayed this prayer in Psalm 51:10-12:

> *Create in me a pure heart, O God, and renew a steadfast spirit within me. Do not cast me from your presence or take your Holy Spirit from me. Restore to me the joy of your salvation and grant me a willing spirit, to sustain me.*

Robert Hampshire from Christianity.com wrote this:

> So, to guard our lives against sin, we must keep the right perspective about who we are… We must not get complacent in our successes. We must saturate our minds with God's Word and invite people in to hold us accountable and encourage us to do good works. We must put practical plans in place to keep our minds, hearts, and bodies pure with prayer and Bible reading, giving others access to our lives, using filters and software… on our devices, scheduling checkpoints with an accountability partner, and putting up barriers to limit our exposure to whatever tempts us the most.

God is always and only trying to get good things to us. But it is up to us to create an environment within our hearts through which good fruit can grow.

Let's surrender the hurt, the bitterness, the pride, and the sin to receive all the good things He has for us.

> *Therefore, confess your sins to one another [your false steps, your offenses], and pray for one another, that you may be healed and restored. The heartfelt and persistent prayer of a righteous man (believer) can accomplish much [when put into action and made effective by God—it is dynamic and can have tremendous power].*
>
> —James 5:16 (AMP)

 **READ**

Look up these Scriptures and write them out, then pray and ask God to reveal to you what they mean for you specifically.

Matthew 5:8

Proverbs 27:19

 **DETOX:**

Ask the Lord to show you any rocks or any sin that you need to dig up and renounce.

Read the following for each rock or sin you listed, plugging it in the blank when you speak: "*I renounce you _____. You are not my master. I put you under the blood of Jesus, so that you are washed away from my life NOW.*"

SELF-REFLECTION:

Is there someone you need to forgive? Is there someone you need to ask to forgive you? Don't wait another day. Forgiveness is so healing and freeing!

- *If you need to forgive*: When someone else knows they have hurt or offended you, it's good for them to hear you tell them that all is forgiven. Go to them in person and release them from it once and for all. However, if they don't know they did something that hurt you, then you can just forgive them in your heart and keep it between you and God.

  Try for restoration in the relationship. If it's not someone you continually need to be around because it's not a healthy relationship or situation, then forgive them and release them, but don't feel that you have to continue in the relationship. It's okay to forgive and then walk away if healthy boundaries are needed.

  In the case of physical or emotional abuse, which can lead to health issues, it's still crucial that you walk free from all bitterness, even though it's not healthy to spend more time with that person. Remember, abuse is never okay, and forgiving someone does not mean permitting someone to abuse you. It does not mean putting yourself or someone else in a harmful situation. I don't want to make blanket statements without saying that you need to seek godly counsel for your specific situation. For instance, you can even ask for another person to be present when you meet to forgive the person who hurt you.

- *If you have hurt someone else*: When you know that you've done something wrong to someone else, or that they were hurt, go to that person immediately and be humble enough to say you're sorry. Ask for forgiveness.

In the case that there's someone you need to apologize to but it's impossible to do that face-to-face, at least do it via a phone call. If you can no longer reach that person, perhaps because they are deceased or you have no contact information for them, still write a letter to them in your journal. (Even though they won't see it, you and God will.) Repent before God of any wrong actions and attitudes toward someone else.

TODAY'S TAKEAWAY:

Tend the soil of your heart and surrender the things to the Lord that can make it a hard place to grow fruit.

PRAYER

Lord, soften my heart. Help me to live so in love with You that the world and its sinful pleasures hold no attraction to me. Help me to keep a soft and pure heart before You. I forgive all those who have hurt me. I surrender any scars. Heal me and help me to only live out of my identity as a child of God.

Day
06

RECLAIM YOUR IDENTITY
STAYING IN
YOUR PURPOSE

DAY 06

One summer, my husband asked me to play in a softball game as part of the co-ed league he had been participating in. They were down a player that day, and I was the last resort, because I don't play sports very well. I reluctantly agreed, mostly to make Jason happy. I was pretty nervous, though! And I got even more nervous as I jogged out onto the field.

Assigned to first base, I stepped on the base and waited as the first pitch was thrown. That pitch was hit hard, a line drive off the bat that hit me right in the SHIN! I stood there stunned for a second as another infielder grabbed the ball that had bounced off of me. But then, I turned to see that the runner was headed straight for me. I didn't know that I was NOT supposed to stand directly on the base! I was supposed to be out of the way so the runner could come through.

Suddenly, I not only had a *throbbing* shin with a huge bruise, but I also had a frustrated runner colliding into me and yelling, "MOVE!" I was in the wrong place. I wasn't in the best place for my skill set to help the team. I did not know how to play first base, thus I was not able to fully help the team win the game. And believe me, that day I suffered the effects of being out of position!

Did you know that there is a place in which God created you to stand? He has gifted you and called you to a destiny for which you are perfectly fashioned. There is a valuable place you were born to occupy. Maybe you aren't really sure what that place is yet, but it's there. You just need to talk to the team Captain and listen for His instructions. Study how to fulfill that purpose to the best of your abilities, so you don't suffer like I did. Haha! You need to know why you were placed on this earth. This becomes even more important when there is pressure applied to your life. Purpose will keep you in place, even when the game of life gets intense.

Purpose is the lifeblood of hope. Purpose gives you a reason to keep moving forward, pursuing greater things. It gives you the will to live when you face insurmountable pain or circumstances. And purpose stems from identity.

The other reason I spend so much time talking about identity with those who are ill is because they need to know *why* they are still here on this earth. When the devil is trying to take them out, they need to know their reason to stay. Have they fulfilled their race, the assignment on their life? Are they satisfied with a long life that fulfilled a purpose? If the answer is no, it's not their time to go.

A godly purpose for living might simply be to raise godly children, which is not so simple in today's world. It might be to create wealth to give to the Gospel through a local church. It might be to champion a cause, create beauty, or change government. Whatever that purpose is, we must stand in it so that we maintain the will to live—not just to survive but to step forward into progress.

It's so important for us to stand in our places of purpose, and even more so if we are attacked with illness. ***While illness is an attack on our physical bodies, purposelessness is an attack on our very existence.*** I find it very interesting that many of the sick people I minister to have experienced some sort of emotional trauma that shook them and discouraged them from their purposes. THEN sickness came in right afterwards. Some have come to a point in their lives where they don't know why they are here. Some have just gone through a divorce or a devastating loss. Some have raised their children and now are empty nesters. Many of them don't know what to look forward to. I always tell them to seek God for their *why*, because He has a reason for them to be here. In fact, it is absolutely essential to discover your *why* in life. Otherwise, it's too easy to give in to whatever pressure comes your way. It's too easy to lose focus, heart, and hope.

Whenever there is lack of vision, purposelessness, or depression, sickness often tries to move in. Why? Because satan knows when we are at our most vulnerable. Lack of vision for the future creates vulnerability that he tries to prey upon. Plus, that aimless living depresses the immune system. We all need a reason to live! The body responds to purpose, vision, activity, and positive usage.

King or Commoner?

In the previous devotion, I shared King David's prayer for God to create in him a clean heart. Let's go back to the beginning of this story and examine the cause.

The reason King David prayed that prayer was because of some very damaging sins he committed. He had just had an affair with a beautiful woman named Bathsheba. The problem was he was a married man and she was also married. After his one-night stand, he later found out she was pregnant. Since her husband had been away at war, David knew Bathsheba was right when she said it was his child. He tried various means to avoid getting caught, which finally ended in having her husband killed on the front line of battle so he could take her as one of his wives. Wow, this was no joke! For someone whom God had once called "a man after his own heart," David obviously was not in a good place.

What happened? How had David's heart gotten so hardened that he was willing to break SIX of the Ten Commandments all at once?

I personally think it all started with him stepping out of his place of identity and purpose, which left him in a place vulnerable to temptation. (See 2 Samuel 11.) You see, it was customary in those days for the king of the nation to lead his troops into battle against a neighboring nation. But instead of acting like the king, David stayed home.

Perhaps he was tired, the pressure got to him, or he became bored, but ultimately, he stepped out of his purpose. Instead of leading as a commander king should, he stayed home like a commoner—an ordinary person. Instead of leading his nation to victory, it seems he lost purpose, got complacent, and stopped living out who he was created to be. He lost his *why*.

That night he walked on the roof of the palace and saw Bathsheba could have been avoided. He was out of his place, kind of like I was when I blocked the runner's path on first base. If David had been leading the army, he would not have been led into temptation.

Besides the fact that he was in the wrong place, David also reacted out of his lowest instinct instead of his high calling. He sent for her instead of resisting temptation. He set aside the fact that he was Israel's moral leader, the God-anointed king of Israel. He wasn't living out of that position. How do I know? Because he would have said to that temptation, "No! That's not who I am. I'm not an adulterer. I'm not a murderer. I'm the *king of Israel,* and therefore, I must protect my family and my kingdom. I must be a good example for the children of my nation. I am God's son, and I want to please Him above all else."

Instead, the king inside of him was silent while the commoner inside of him spoke up and said, "*Yes, I can go ahead and take what I want.*"

When we lose our *why*—the purpose for which we are placed here on this earth—we start acting like commoners. We listen to our lowest instincts instead of our high calling. We stop leading life and start being led by carnal desires. We stop standing in our identities, on the offensive against the enemy, and we start giving in, growing complacent, and staying home, so to speak. We start allowing things inside our homes that were never meant to be there.

But when we fight for our God-anointed purposes, it will propel us toward healthy attitudes, actions, appetites, and accountability.

There was a point in my life when I had lost my *why*. I felt like sickness had taken over my dreams. I started doubting my destiny. I stopped dreaming, stopped pursuing, and stopped creating. I didn't go on the offensive against the enemies of self-hatred and sickness. Instead, I "stayed home," acted like a commoner, and felt sorry for myself. I knew I was called to lead worship and to teach the Word of God, to be a wife and a mother, but I had let go of my identity, my *why*. I stopped fighting for God's best, because I didn't believe *I* was His best. I had fallen off the cliff into unbelief and hopelessness. I didn't go to war against the enemy of my soul. Instead, I didn't even put up a fight.

They say that if someone loses the will to live, no doctor can help them. People lose the will to live because they lose sight of their *why*, their created purpose.

Thankfully, through Jesus we have hope and a future, according to Jeremiah 29:11. We have a reason to live that is important, eternal, and urgent, as outlined in Isaiah 61 and Mark 16:15. It's crucial to keep that *why* in front of our eyes when life gets tough or when pain is shouting. We must not wander aimlessly and let the devil tempt us. We must stand up and march out to battle! Why? Because we are not commoners. We are kings. And we represent the King of Kings.

Reversing Course

Even when/if we do wander off or give up on our purposes, God is so faithful to send out a search party. God sent the prophet Nathan to confront David and pull him back into position. Nathan reminded David of who he was, which dictated how he should have acted. When David realized the horrible evil in his own heart, he humbled himself before the Lord and deeply repented. God was merciful, as He is with us all. In fact, later in the Bible, David was still called "a man of faith" by the apostle Paul (Hebrews 11).

The point is, David's sin was the result of a progression of choices, starting with stepping outside of his *why*—his created purpose and God-anointed identity as king and moral leader of Israel. My personal sins of unbelief and self-hatred were the result of listening to the wrong voices and letting go of my own *why*. There were many others throughout the Bible who took steps outside of their identities, and yet God was always faithful to restore and forgive.

Why did Samson, a powerful man with God-given strength, sin with a temptress named Delilah, who did not love God? It's because he forgot who he was: a Nazarite called before he was even born to deliver the Israelites from the Philistines. And yet, even though he was taken prisoner because Delilah betrayed him to the Philistines, Samson still delivered the Israelites by pushing down the pillars that supported the Philistines' temple while they were in it, and it killed all of their evil leaders. God still gave Samson the chance to fulfill his destiny once he repented.

Why did the apostle Peter deny knowing Jesus on the night Jesus was arrested? Because he stepped out of his place as a disciple of Jesus and into a place of fear. But even so, Peter repented, was forgiven, and was later used in a mighty way to preach a message that got thousands born again on the Day of Pentecost. He went on to become the central disciple in reaching the Jewish nation for Jesus.

Why did the newly-freed children of Israel worship a golden idol instead of their God, who delivered them from Egyptian slavery? They forgot who they were, a chosen people and the children of the Deliverer. And still, God always had compassion on them and forgave their sins.

The point is, it's never too late to step back into your created purpose. It's never too late to do what God has called you to do. Until you're dead, it's never too late.

Your Job Description

What has God called you to do that you have set aside or rejected?

Have you allowed things to pull you out of your *why*? Has it affected your will to live? Do you find yourself wondering if there's still time for you to fulfill the mandate on your life?

If you don't know why you are here, let me start with something that we're ALL called to do, as spelled out to every believer in Matthew 28:18-20:

> *Then Jesus came to them and said, "All authority in heaven and on earth has been given to me. Therefore go and make disciples of all nations, baptizing them in the name of the Father and of the Son and of the Holy Spirit, and teaching them to obey everything I have commanded you. And surely I am with you always, to the very end of the age."*

Telling others about Jesus and discipling them in Truth is our MAIN job description here on Earth. The details of HOW we each fulfill that mandate is just the car we drive on our assignment. Everything we do as an occupation is actually just a vehicle to carry the Good News to others. Here are some of the other titles in your job description here on Earth:

> *But you are a <u>chosen people</u>, a <u>royal priesthood</u>, a <u>holy nation</u>, <u>God's special possession</u>, that you may <u>declare the praises of him who called you</u> out of darkness into his wonderful light.*
> —1 Peter 2:9

If we all used this as our mission statement, to declare God's praises and make disciples, we would all be very busy. We have job security, and there is no issue with others occupying the space we were created to fill, because the harvest is plentiful, but the harvesters are too few (Matthew 9:37). God needs all of us to speak to the people He has placed in our realm of influence about Him, whether that's our kids or our coworkers. That is the greatest purpose any of us could have. People need to be our *why*.

Stay in your purpose and let it propel you toward a more hopeful tomorrow, brimming with possibility. Your *why* will push you forward in this journey to health. Your *why* will give you the will to live. Your *why* will keep you busy about your Father's business. Each moment of each day is a gift that we spend on something. Remember that each day can count toward building people, who are eternal. Don't be like King David and step out of position to be like the commoners around you. Let's be kings who point others to the King of Kings!

Look up and meditate on Romans 12:1-21 and Isaiah 61.

Have you allowed anything—such as sickness, wrong beliefs about yourself, or what other people have said about you—to pull you out of your destiny? Have you accepted titles or job descriptions that don't fit your created purpose? Call them out! Make this declaration: "No! That's not who I am. I'm not a _____. I'm a royal priest of God, and therefore I must protect that calling with everything."

SELF-REFLECTION:

What's your *why*? Write down the callings of God on your life, the why behind Him placing you here for such a time as this. If you know the specifics of how you are called to fulfill the Great Commission, write those down. If you aren't sure, look at Isaiah 61 and Mark 16:15, plus reread any words spoken over your life or giftings God has given you.

 # TODAY'S TAKEAWAY:

I will stay in my created purpose to avoid getting derailed by distractions, discouragement, or sin. And if I don't yet know what that purpose is, I will ask God to show me each step I'm to take.

PRAYER

Holy Spirit, reveal to me ways that I have stepped away from my anointing and purpose. Reveal my why so that I can pursue it and let it propel me toward the fight instead of hanging back. Help me to step back into the center of Your will in every area of my life so that healing and grace can flow through my life to those around me.

RECLAIM YOUR IDENTITY

DITCH THE T.R.A.F.F.I.C.

DAY 07

It's day seven, and I pray that this week has been filled with revelation from the Holy Spirit, encouragement for your soul, and freedom from some things that have been weighing you down. Great job taking action and sticking with it! I hope you have been taking your Daily Faith Boosters (as discussed at the beginning of this book) like medicine, along with reading each day's devotion. I'm excited to see all that God is going to do in this next week. Keep speaking your healing Scriptures, immersing your life with healing teaching, and turning off any messages of fear.

Let's continue our study on identity, because it has so much to do with where we are headed in life.

Speaking of heading somewhere, one time my family was on a road trip to go out West, but we had timed the drive badly. You see, we hit the wonderful city of Chicago just in time for rush hour traffic. I have never seen anything quite like it! We sat in bumper-to-bumper traffic from one end of Chicago to the other for TWO HOURS. It was the most maddening thing. Just when we thought we were in the clear, another accident with another jam would come into view.

Has your life ever felt like that? Have you ever felt stuck? Like you're making no progress? Perhaps you've been praying for change, and it just isn't coming? Maybe it feels like your purpose and destiny have been derailed? Perhaps you've been seeking change, not just in the area of health but also in other areas of your life. Maybe you really connected to the devotion on day six in which we talked about purpose and destiny because you feel so trapped where you are. If so, you're not alone.

Today we are diving into the things that get in our way on our journey to our destinies.

If you're anything like me, you hate traffic! It feels so pointless to sit there blocked in by cars that aren't moving. I think many Christians have forgotten their salvation and let a few choice words fly while in traffic. Haha!

Maybe you feel like you're in a traffic jam on the highway of life. You want free from it, yet you feel powerless to move those other cars out of the way. That's the way we get in life when we allow the mental T.R.A.F.F.I.C. to stop us from getting home to Kingdom living. Here's what the acronym stands for.

T.R.A.F.F.I.C.

Thought patterns - We must break wrong patterns of thinking in order to believe what God says about us. If we can identify our three most predominant thoughts throughout our day, we can see where we're headed. Out of our thoughts come beliefs in our hearts, and out of our beliefs in our hearts, our mouths speak. Those words and beliefs steer our lives, like the rudder of a ship, but they start with thoughts.

The only way to change our thoughts is by renewing our minds with the Word of God (Romans 12:2, Ephesians 5:26). Find a few Scriptures that pertain to recurring bad thoughts you've been having, and write them down. Thoughts become strongholds of belief that can hold us back until we allow God to tear down that wall, brick by brick. Negative thoughts keep us bumper-to-bumper with other negative thinkers, stuck.

Rocks - We've already devoted a day to this topic, but here's our reminder to continue digging up those rocks of bitterness, offense, pride, sin, and anything else that causes our hearts to grow calloused and hard. Rocks will puncture our tires on the road of life, making forward progress very difficult. Remember, these are modes of operation that build strongholds in our lives. Hardened hearts cause us to make bad decisions. Rocks can also cause sickness in our bodies, because they shut out the light, which brings rot to what would otherwise be a healthy heart. They disease the soul. See the parable of the sower from Matthew 13.

It is such a wonderful thing to be delivered from those things that have built up in the deep places of the soul. Sometimes rocks may be too deep for us to even see without the Holy Spirit's counsel. Pray and ask Him to show you what they are, and then start renouncing them. If there is a deliverance ministry at your church, it's also great to receive prayer over these areas from godly leaders.

Attitudes - We all know the ones. That bad funk we get into. The looks we throw at spouses like daggers. The complaining we annoy our coworkers with. Did you know that attitudes are paths we take? When we wake up and have a resentful attitude toward our spouse, it's because we are facing in the wrong direction, headed down a path of unforgiveness and selfishness.

Maybe it starts off innocently enough. "Well, what about me? Doesn't he care?" I huff under my breath as I give my husband the side-eye when he sits down to watch his favorite show. With my passive aggressive attitude, I *think* I am just making sure he knows I'm not happy. But in that moment, what I'm actually doing is walking in the opposite direction of love. Maybe we get into an argument over what each of us wants, which leads to personal attacks and hurt feelings. It's a path neither of us wanted to go down. And I made the first move by setting the direction of our evening with my attitude.

To change directions, we must confront wrong attitudes/ directions in order to turn our lives back toward Jesus. Attitudes stem from beliefs. Do you believe your spouse doesn't love you? Do you believe there's no hope? That nothing will change? That no one cares about you? No one understands you or appreciates you? Then you are going in the wrong direction! You must repent of any attitudes that keep you from loving God, loving others, and loving yourself, in that order.

Study how Jesus acted and the attitude He carried in every situation. He always faced Himself toward the center of God's will as He endured betrayal, persecution, loneliness, and dark times.

Tip: Ask a close friend, mentor, or your spouse to be your "attitude barometer" if you're serious about change. Accountability is key to getting unstuck when you're in a mental traffic jam going the wrong direction!

Familiar Spirits - Let's talk about family stuff that's hanging around from our old corrupted DNAs—you know, our pre-Jesus days. Or maybe we were affected by the choices our parents made, and how they raised us has built a framework through which we see the world. Have you ever met someone who was raised in a very dysfunctional environment? Often, they have social abnormalities, weird behaviors, or strange reactions to situations. But to them, it feels completely normal. For some, never having enough money feels normal. For others, being in abusive relationships unfortunately feels like their normal. And still others find that they are living in a prison of fear, and yet it feels like home.

Those familiar spirits mask their voices so that they sound like YOU. They feel so normal and almost create a false sense of security. But they are actually demonic familiar spirits.

For me, the spirits of rejection and shame felt so much like my own voice and thoughts that I had lost my own voice. I would repeat what I heard that spirit saying to me, and it felt like my own thoughts. But it wasn't me saying those bad things about myself; it was lying spirits I needed to renounce.

Perhaps your "family album" includes relatives such as "Great Uncle Rejection," "Granny Greed," "Daddy Diabetes," "Aunt Adultery," "Papa Poverty," "Mama Martyrdom," and so on.

Take time to think about and write down those voices that may be familiar but aren't from God. Unmasking them is the first step to revoking their power in your life. Here are some hints to unmasking familiar spirits:

1. If a thought brings emotional pain, confusion, and turmoil, it could be a familiar spirit.
2. If a label or curse was spoken over you by a family member and now you're living it out, it's a familiar spirit.
3. If you see some of the same dysfunction in your life that your parents struggled with, it could be a familiar spirit. This is why children of alcoholics sometimes fall into the same pit as their parents, even though they always said they would never touch alcohol. It's because they ran to the familiar, just like the children of Israel wanted to do when they asked to go back to Egypt instead of advancing to the Promised Land. They were afraid, and when life got unpredictable, they wanted what was familiar.
4. If there seems to be a glass ceiling that you just can't break through due to fear, it's possibly a familiar spirit.
5. If you often sabotage your own success, just like one of your parents did, it's a familiar spirit.

We all grew up with a tainted view of life because we were born in this sin fallen world. And no matter how hard our parents tried, we all acquired a few childhood scars. Most of the time, we get stuck from a very young age in these familiar patterns that keep us in T.R.A.F.F.I.C. That's why we must

THE 30-DAY HEALING DARE

ask God for our new normal. The more familiar we grow with the voice of the Holy Spirit, the less familiar those other voices will feel. We must renounce those evil spirits that have tormented us for far too long and command them to go, in the name of Jesus! If Jesus is our master, we will not follow the voice of another.

Fear - The second F in T.R.A.F.F.I.C stands for fear. Fear is a huge part of the curse that came upon the earth after Adam sinned. Fear is simply faith in the wrong thing. It is a belief that the wrong things are going to happen instead of believing that what God says is going to happen. There is fear of failure, fear of rejection, fear of punishment, fear of loss, fear of lack, and fear manifesting as worry, anxiety, panic, nervousness, timidity, shyness, self-deprecation, etc. It takes different forms, but all of it must bow to the name of Jesus!

I devote an entire day to defeating fear, but in the meantime, look up 2 Timothy 1:7 and start confessing it daily. Then tell fear, "I command you to leave now, in the name of Jesus!" Pay no attention to your emotions when those symptoms of fear start to creep up, but instead, boldly and confidently command fear to hit the road! It has absolutely no choice but to go if you stand your ground. Stop owning and accepting it as yours, and start recognizing it for the defeated foe that it is. Jesus defeated fear! Fear cannot keep you stuck any longer!

Identity Thieves - These are names, labels, and word curses that you've accepted as "you." They are ungodly mirages that mask your true self-worth. And they sabotage your success every time things start to get better. They are distortions of the real you. They can be seemingly harmless names, such as "fat," "dumb," or "clumsy," and they can be very destructive names, such as "unworthy," "unwanted," "broken," and "worthless."

All of us have painful memories of being called a bad name, but some of us have internalized and taken on that identity. For instance, many men were told by their fathers that they couldn't do anything right, and now as adults, they find themselves paralyzed. They sabotage their success anytime things start going right. Why? They are living out of that wrong identity. Listen, *you don't need anyone's permission to be successful, happy, or free*. God gave you permission to walk in freedom and to be who He says you are. (Side note: If you haven't seen the movies, *I Can Only Imagine* and *Courageous,* you need to watch them! They are both good illustrations of these points.)

Write down the bad names you call yourself, along with the ones others said that hurt the most, and then command every one of those names to bow to the name of Jesus! Say, "I am no longer answering to this name anymore!" I would even go so far as to burn the paper you write those bad names on, as a symbol that you are free from them. These are deep ruts on your road, and they need to be repaired in order for you to pick up speed once again. Fill the potholes and ruts with the new names God calls you. He calls you wonderful, awesome, and able. He adores you and thinks you are fabulous! So start acting like the person your Father says you are.

Condemnation - Condemnation constantly says, "You are hopeless." It makes us feel like no one else has ever done something so bad. It tells us there's no path to restoration, that we can never measure up. Condemning oneself or someone else is a form of unforgiveness and judgment. When we condemn ourselves, we are ignoring the REAL Judge's verdict. Jesus is Judge of the universe, and He calls us innocent when we receive His pardon. Imagine Him stepping in and taking that sin, that reason we feel we aren't good enough. He took it upon Himself when He carried the sins of the world to the cross, and He buried those things with Him in the grave. When He rose again, He gave us a brand-new start. He gave us His perfection, His good name, His reputation, His power, His authority, His royalty, His holiness, and His worthiness. We are no longer condemned! Romans 8:1-2 say:

Therefore, there is now no condemnation for those who are in Christ Jesus, because through Christ Jesus the law of the Spirit who gives life has set you free from the law of sin and death.

A woman caught in adultery was brought to Jesus, and when everyone wanted to stone her, He told the crowd, "He who is without sin, cast the first stone." Everyone was convicted and walked away. And here's what Jesus said to her:

Jesus straightened up and asked her, "Woman, where are they? Has no one condemned you?" "No one, sir," she said. "Then neither do I condemn you," Jesus declared. "Go now and leave your life of sin."

—John 8:10-11.

Friend, you CAN be free of the T.R.A.F.F.I.C. that has held you in place for far too long. It's time to get back on the road and enjoy the journey with Jesus. It's time to take the outer belt to your destiny, free of the world's roadblocks and the devil's holdups.

This is an in-depth devotion that may take some time to pray through and process, but it will be worth it. So put on some worship music, read through the list again, and start praying about where you are stuck. Ask the Holy Spirit's power to fill you and revive you with new strength to throw off the things that have kept you stuck. Ditch the T.R.A.F.F.I.C.!

 **READ**

Look up 1 Peter 2:1-5 and write it out in first person:

DETOX:

Write about the T.R.A.F.F.I.C. that you are giving to Jesus today. Surrender it all and ask the Holy Spirit to do a work within you. He is faithful to reveal, heal, and deliver!

 # SELF-REFLECTION:

Most of this devotion is a mirror into your life, so take time to really pray through each item and thank God for freedom in that area.

 # TODAY'S TAKEAWAY:

I will not get bogged down by the T.R.A.F.F.I.C. of life. I receive the freedom of the Holy Spirit in my spirit, soul, and body.

PRAYER

Jesus, thank You for helping me to ditch all of the T.R.A.F.F.I.C. that has been holding me back. You have set me free, so I am free indeed! I renounce every demonic stronghold, lie, and attitude that is not of You. I pull up roots from my heart so my soil grows good things. I see who You call me in your Word, and I choose to walk in that identity and not the identity of this world's system!

RECLAIM YOUR IDENTITY

THE LAW
OF LOVE

DAY 08

J esus gave us one commandment that sums up everything that really matters in life:

> *Jesus replied: "Love the Lord your God with all your heart and with all your soul and with all your mind. This is the first and greatest commandment. And the second is like it: Love your neighbor as yourself. All the Law and the Prophets hang on these two commandments."*
>
> —Matthew 22:37-40

This is the law of love, and within it is contained the power to fulfill every other commandment. The law of love cannot be violated without consequences, even if that violation is toward ourselves. Why? Because anything not done in love is done outside of God's Kingdom. When we operate outside of love, we are operating in that other kingdom, the realm of darkness and evil. The Bible says that God IS love, and so if we are living in Him, we are living in love itself:

> *And so we know and rely on the love God has for us. God is love. Whoever lives in love lives in God, and God in them.*
>
> —1 John 4:16

As I detail in *Healed Overnight: Five Steps to Accessing Supernatural Healing*, I lived with hatred toward myself for years. Essentially, I was breaking the law of love against myself. The root of this self-hatred was both shame and pride. Now that sounds like an oxymoron, but I would think thoughts that aligned with one or the other of these roots.

Shame

"I'm not good enough," is the predominant thought that shame speaks, and hopelessness is its predominant outcome. It is a spirit that brings rejection, unworthiness, isolation, loneliness, hopelessness, depression, and even suicide. It makes people want to hide. It is the feeling that one is inherently flawed or hopeless. It makes us feel like something is wrong with us, that we just can't get it together. It makes us afraid to ask for help for fear of being found lacking. It constantly wants us to compare ourselves to others. We never measure up when we do this.

Shame causes women to stay in abusive relationships because they feel it is their fault or that they aren't worthy of better treatment. Shame makes people withdraw or lash out in relationships. Shame shows up looking like low self-esteem, but it runs the gamut all the way to suicide and depression, because of the hopelessness it causes.

Shame is nothing to mess with. In fact, Adam and Eve's first symptom from the Fall was shame. We know this because they immediately went and hid themselves so God could not find them (Genesis 3:8-10). I dealt with it for years in the form of self-hatred, body image issues, fear of confessing my faults, and more. I'm so glad I've been set free!

Pride

On the other hand, we have pride. The thought that "I must *earn* love" is rooted in pride. Pride is all about self-righteousness, or trying to make oneself good enough through works. "If it's gonna be, it's up to me" is one of pride's mantras. Another one is "I don't need anyone." Pride cannot accept fault or responsibility, and it certainly doesn't like to apologize. Pride obliterates relationships because of that lack of vulnerability. Pride and shame work hand in hand. Since I desperately wanted to be accepted and worthy of love, I would perform and work so hard to be perfect, to be good enough, to prove my loyalty to people, or to defend my decisions. I leaned on my own strengths and did things in my own ability instead of relying on God. This independence apart from God is pride.

Pride says, "I cannot be wrong or make mistakes because that would make me unworthy. So I will defend myself, never admit fault or failure, and never humble myself to receive correction." For me, I always had an ongoing inward dialogue that made me do mental gymnastics. I was worried about what others would perceive as my motives. One of the worst things that could happen to me was being misunderstood. I was terrified of upsetting anyone. I avoided conflict like the plague, and thus I did not open myself to deep relationships.

Pride exalts its own preservation over the will and desires of the Holy Spirit. It tries to accuse and condemn *others* in an effort to make itself feel better. Pride stands in opposition to love, because love is not boastful or proud (1 Corinthians 13:4). It can make someone very legalistic, judgmental, and unforgiving. *By justifying itself, it cannot receive the justification that comes by faith in Jesus*:

> *Know that a person is not justified by the works of the law, but by faith in Jesus Christ. So we, too, have put our faith in Christ Jesus that we may be justified by faith in Christ and not by the works of the law, because by the works of the law no one will be justified.*
>
> —Galatians 2:16

Both shame and pride do not allow us to forgive ourselves if we make a mistake, at least not without feeling miserable and punishing ourselves for a time. Both shame and pride break the law of love and are modes of operation that are destructive forces. You may ask, "Amy, what does all this have to do with physical healing?" Spiritual and emotional health have EVERYTHING to do with physical health. Shame and pride both have the power to break down physical bodies and bring on symptoms that range from migraine headaches, digestive issues, and muscle aches to M.S., strokes, and heart disease.

How? Because without love, a human body deteriorates. Several studies have shown that babies who do not receive human touch and affection, although still fed and diapered, fail to thrive and often die. *Love is an inborn basic necessity for survival.* Thankfully, we have a Father who is ready and waiting to shower us with His lavish, overwhelming, all-encompassing love! It's still up to us to receive it, instead of blocking it out of our lives.

Have you been breaking the law of love against yourself?

Do you recognize some of these issues in your own heart?

Do you hear shame-filled thoughts and arguments in your head?

Do you kill relationships because of pride?

Then let's take a look at the cure.

The Cure

A radical encounter with Love, Himself started my journey toward letting go of the roots of shame and pride.

One night at a youth camp when I was 19 years old, I found myself on my face before Jesus, and His love felt like liquid warmth being poured over me. It was a very tangible feeling, and it filled all the broken places in me. He held me close and started to heal the rejection that I had felt for so many years.

It took several years before I could fully love myself, but that night I KNEW that at least *He* loved me. I even wrote a song to the Lord as a vow, the chorus of which says:

> *I'm gonna live like You are enough for me.*
> *I'm gonna live like Your love has made me free.*
> *No matter what this whole world may say or think,*
> *I'm gonna live like You are enough for me.*
> *Jesus, You, only You are enough for me.*

The answer—the cure—for pride and shame is spending time with Love, Himself and letting His worthiness, justification, and acceptance heal all the brokenness. His love is the most powerful force in the universe! Nothing will ever make Him stop loving you.

Many of God's children are living life in a love deficit, because they have not fully allowed God to love them, nor have they opened their hearts to let others love them. They feel constant pain in their hearts and questions about their worth in their heads. They feel they must earn love, perform for love, or appear strong like they don't need love.

Many times, someone's relationship with their earthly father affects their view of God's love. But all of these misconceptions and love deficits are simply blown away when we get into God's presence and hear what He thinks about us.

When I first started my journey toward accepting myself, I felt the Lord whisper to me, "Ask Me what I think of you." So I did, replying, "All right, Jesus, what do You think of me?" I expected a list of things I needed to do better, or sins I needed to stop committing. Instead, I got a long list of the things God loves about me personally. He even had special nicknames for me. It was so completely shocking that I couldn't believe He was the One saying it, thinking it was just my own thoughts. But the next day, a friend gave me a card that said, "When I was praying for you yesterday, I felt like God was saying all of this about you," and it listed many of the same things in the same words that I had heard in my spirit the night before. I still cry when I read that card all these years later. How great is the Father's love for us!

You *do* know that He thinks ONLY good thoughts toward you, right? He fully and completely adores you. He passionately and adamantly defends you. He willingly extends mercy when you fail. He is not angry with you. He only seeks to do good to you. Will you receive the powerful love of your Father? Will you accept the fact that He cherishes and values and honors you? Isaiah 54:10 (ESV) says:

> *"For the mountains may depart and the hills be removed, but my steadfast love shall not depart from you, and my covenant of peace shall not be removed," says the Lord, who has compassion on you.*

What sweetness to know that His love is a constant force, strong enough to pull us out of the deepest of despair. How much does God love you? John 17:23 shares a prayer Jesus prayed to the Father:

> *I in them and you in me—so that they may be brought to complete unity. Then the world will know that you sent me and <u>have loved them even as you have loved me</u>.*

Perhaps the most shocking of all truths in the Bible is this: that God loves us just as much as He loves Jesus.

Take time to write out and speak 1 John 4:8-19:

Write about the areas in yourself where you recognize you need God's love.

SELF-REFLECTION:

Find a few Scriptures that speak directly to the areas where you have been breaking the law of love, toward yourself or toward others, and journal about them.

 # TODAY'S TAKEAWAY:

I will break free from the cycles of pride and shame by keeping the law of love.

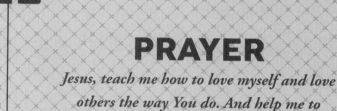

PRAYER

Jesus, teach me how to love myself and love others the way You do. And help me to love You and honor Your voice in my life above all else.

RECLAIM YOUR IDENTITY

IT'S A NEW DAY, BABY!

DAY 09

B *ut those who embraced him and took hold of his name were given authority to become the children of God!*

—John 1:12 (TPT)

I have so enjoyed being a mother to my beautiful children, partly because I get to see the world from fresh pairs of eyes. When my two-year-old discovers the funny elephants at the zoo and squeals with delight, it's like I'm looking at elephants for the first time also. And it's so sweet to see the world through the perspective of an innocent child.

Did you know that's how God wants us to see ourselves? Kids don't have identity issues until life knocks them around and they suffer disappointments, setbacks, or bullying. Kids see themselves as superheroes, astronauts, and rock stars. Even jobs that adults see as unglamorous seem exciting to a kid; garbage truck drivers, mothers, and grocery store cashiers all seem like cool jobs to kids!

Life may have knocked you down many times and damaged your identity. But did you know that when you were born again, you were translated out of that old kingdom of darkness, and you became alive spiritually in the earth as a completely new person?

You now have a new name with new spiritual DNA! You became a brand-new, alive version of yourself!

It's a new day, baby! God changed our names from "Lost and Guilty" to "Found and Forgiven" when we asked Him to be our Father. When we willingly chose to become bound to Him as our partner for life, we were separated from darkness:

He has delivered us from the power of darkness and conveyed us into the kingdom of the Son of His love.

—Colossians 1:13 (NKJV)

That darkness includes sickness, fear, poverty, depression, addiction, and every evil work. Sickness cannot survive in the light *unless* we dim the light inside of us.

When we fully embrace our identities as Father God's beloved children, the world takes on a new perspective. We CAN see ourselves differently. And it impacts how we act, think, and feel. Think about this:

- Your Daddy owns it all.
- Your Daddy is bigger and stronger than all circumstances.
- Your Daddy makes evil run in terror.
- Your Daddy is fiercely passionate about your success.
- Your Daddy has given you HIS authority, because you are His kid!
- **You belong to Him, so sickness does NOT belong in you!**

Sickness is a corruption of your spiritual identity. It goes against who you are as God's healthy child, with nothing missing and nothing broken! (And that's where ENFORCING your God-given rights comes in, but that's a topic for another day.) When you were adopted into God's household (Ephesians 1:5), you received His spiritual DNA. You received a transfusion of spiritual light into your darkened heart. You no longer belong to the night. You belong to the day! You are no longer doomed to wander as an orphan, in loneliness and with loss of identity. You have the BEST Dad and the best family lineage anyone could ask for.

It's Already Covered

Let's take a moment to talk about the sacrifice Jesus made. We need to be reminded daily of what He paid for, because it covered everything. Jesus had to shed His blood to pay for our sins because life is in the blood. The Bible says:

> He is despised and rejected by men, a Man of sorrows and acquainted with grief. And we hid, as it were, our faces from Him; He was despised, and we did not esteem Him. Surely He has borne our griefs and carried our sorrows; yet we esteemed Him stricken, smitten by God, and afflicted.
>
> But He was wounded for our transgressions, He was bruised for our iniquities; the chastisement for our peace was upon Him, and by His stripes we are healed.
>
> —Isaiah 53:3-5 (NKJV)

Jesus took rejection so we could be accepted. He was despised and had insults and shame hurled at Him so that we could be perfectly loved. He paid for our peace with His chastisement (meaning severe criticism; a rebuke or strong reprimand, corporal punishment; a beating, according to dictionary.com). He had a Roman whip, an instrument of torture, hurled at His skin and ripped from it over and over again. The beating He received is described as:

> Just as many were appalled at the sight of him (for so marred was his appearance, like an object of horror; <u>he no longer looked like a man</u>), so now he will startle many nations. Kings will be shocked speechless before him.
>
> —Isaiah 52:14-15a (TPT)

Jesus was so destroyed by that whip, people couldn't even tell He was a man anymore. His identity was stripped from Him completely. The soldiers even mocked His identity. Think about that! He could no longer be identified SO THAT YOU AND I COULD HAVE A RESTORATION OF IDENTITY and we could belong! This is how much He took for you and for me. Thank you, Jesus!

He paid for the spiritual cure to every root of physical pain, mental torment, and spiritual illness—every category of disease. Bill Winston says it this way:

> "When Jesus got beat, every lash represented one of the major categories of diseases or disorders. When you get healing from God, it comes from the Spirit and it destroys the ground in which the sickness is embedded. The soldiers said, 'If you are the son of God, take yourself down from there.' But He gave his life—no one killed Him—He gave His life so that we could come back to the Father."

Can you see Him, willingly going to the cross, knowing what He would have to endure, and yet seeing us in the future? It was His love for us that compelled Him to become separated from His Father so that we could be reunited with Him. Breathtaking! Oh, how I love this passage that further explains what Jesus's sacrifice did for us:

> *For we've been buried with him into his death. Our "baptism into death" also means <u>we were raised with him when we believed in God's resurrection power</u>, the power that raised him from death's realm. <u>This "realm of death" describes our former state</u>, for we were held in sin's grasp. <u>But now, we've</u>*

THE 30-DAY HEALING DARE

been resurrected out of that "realm of death" never to return, for we are forever alive and forgiven of all our sins!

He canceled out every legal violation we had on our record and the old arrest warrant that stood to indict us. He erased it all— our sins, our stained soul—he deleted it all and they cannot be retrieved! Everything we once were in Adam has been placed onto his cross and nailed permanently there as a public display of cancellation.

Then Jesus made a public spectacle of all the powers and principalities of darkness, stripping away from them every weapon and all their spiritual authority and power to accuse us. And by the power of the cross, Jesus led them around as prisoners in a procession of triumph. He was not their prisoner; they were his!
—Colossians 2:12-15 (TPT)

Praise God, He made a way for a whole new you! It's a new day, baby! And it's time to start living out of YOUR new identity, bought and paid for with the blood of Jesus. The apostle John said this:

Behold what manner of love the Father has bestowed on us, that we should be called children of God! Therefore the world does not know us, because it did not know Him.
—1 John 3:1 (NKJV)

Jesus was rejected by the world so that we could be accepted by God. He gave us brand-new DNA!

It Is NOT "Part of Who You Are"

As God's child, with His DNA, sickness doesn't fit in your picture. Sickness is a distortion and violation of your physical genetic make-up AND your spiritual genetic makeup. Now, that doesn't mean the devil won't TRY to come in with something that violates your God-given identity. But it does mean you do not have to allow sickness to REMAIN. You have a right to stand in your new identity as a healthy, whole, and strong person.

However, if you internalize that sickness, allow it to become PART of you or who you think you are, and accept it as your new normal, it has a right to remain.

It can propagate throughout your body and your soul. It is still an illegal violation of your covenant rights, but you have *legally allowed* it to stay through your acceptance of the facts OVER the truth of God's Word.

For sickness to stay and eventually bring death, it has to have permission from you. You may say, "I certainly have not given it permission to stay in me!" But perhaps you have simply through mental assent or silence. Permission might sound something like, "Yes, I have cancer," "Diabetes runs in my family," "High blood pressure is just something I have to cope with," "*My* anxiety," or "I am gaining weight, like most women my age."

Sickness, like sin, has a way of sneaking in slowly through a subtle twisting of thought and attitude. We give in or call it normal when we claim it as our own. Stop labeling yourself according to a disease, because you are NOT that disease. Stop calling yourself a "diabetic" or an "alcoholic" or a "fall risk." Start calling yourself healed!

It's time for you to start living out of your new identity, speaking ONLY the things that line up with who Father God says you are.

<table>
<tr><td>

Stop saying:

"I am sick."

"I am in pain."

"I am ugly."

"I am tired."

"I am lonely/forgotten."

</td><td>

Start saying:

"I am healed."

"I am in Christ."

"I am God's masterpiece."

"I am vibrant and strong."

"I am loved."

</td></tr>
</table>

Start living out of the REAL you, who God says you are!

 READ

Meditate on Ephesians 2:19 (NKJV):

> *Now, therefore, you are no longer strangers and foreigners, but fellow citizens with the saints and members of the household of God.*

 DETOX:

As we head into the next section of this devotional, a great way to detox anything else that the Holy Spirit wants to remove is through a fast.

A fast is not to move God but to move ourselves. It is to eliminate distractions and quiet our flesh, so we hear His voice clearly.

So, here's your dare: Fast *something* for seven days, whether that is media, food, sugar, caffeine, or something else that is distracting you or creates a strong appetite in your flesh. (Obviously, make sure that it is physically safe for you to fast food, and if it isn't, choose something else.) If you are physically able to fast food in some way, I highly recommend it, but check with your doctor if there's a question of whether your body is okay to do that.

When I was sick, I knew I needed to hear from God as to why, so I did a liquid fast for seven days. It wasn't hard after the second day! During the last five days, after I got over feeling super hungry, it felt like the voice of God was ten times louder. That was when I got my "marching orders" for receiving my healing!

I pray that as you choose a fast, the Holy Spirit will reveal to you His great desire for you to be healed, as well as anything that is blocking that healing from manifesting.

TESTIMONY:

"Hi! You prayed for a complete restoration of my identity last year. Thank you for praying for me! See the pictures of me dancing? This is so much progress! This is the first time I put on ballet clothes and pointe shoes in about 10 years. I decided when I was all alone to try in faith. I have not seen myself like this for many years. Thank you!"

—LISA

TODAY'S TAKEAWAY:

I have a brand new identity in Jesus. Healed is part of who I am!

PRAYER

Jesus, thank You that as I fast and pray, You will reveal your perfect will in my life, that You will direct my steps, give me answers, and remove anything that should not be in my heart. Father, I am Yours. Father, I belong to You.

REPAINT YOUR PICTURE

WRITING THE VISION

DAY 10

hen there is no clear prophetic vision, people quickly wander astray. But when you follow the revelation of the Word, heaven's bliss fills your soul.

—Proverbs 29:18 (TPT)

Okay, we have spent some time covering our first step in receiving healing, which is:

1. Reclaim your identity. (Know who you are in Christ.)

Now, it's time to move on to step two, which is:

2. Repaint your picture.

During my own 30-day Healing Dare, this was a big revelation for me, because I believed this was just the way I was, so therefore, I could not SEE anything different. For several years, I could not envision myself as whole and well. All I saw was what stared back at me in the mirror. I had no clear vision, so I sat moping about how my body felt or looked. I sank into despair over the seemingly hopeless situation. All the while, the Word of God was yelling Truth. Was I listening? Not until I got desperate. And angry. And just done with staying stuck.

There will come a moment when the pain of staying the same is greater than the pain of change. It's in that moment we hopefully make the decision to change. We are ready to receive a new vision. The Holy Spirit can come in and show us what is possible through Him. That's exactly where I found myself when I started a seven-day fast during the eighth year of being ill in my body.

I was done. I had been married almost a year. I wanted children. And I was very tired of feeling terrible all the time. I had talked myself out of change for a long time. I had found comfort in the fact that there were others who were also going through physical issues, and I wasn't alone. I had hung back and pushed back until I could no longer stand the way I was living on the inside. **That confinement of unbelief was TOO SMALL. The view was terrible. It was time for a new picture.**

I turned to God's Word and to other people's testimonies to start to imagine what was possible for myself. I needed something to pull my heart into agreement with a future that was bigger than was naturally possible. I needed a miracle.

If you find yourself needing a miracle (a miracle being something that defies the natural realm but is very much normal in God's supernatural realm), then listen up.

Today is your day for change. But it starts with a brand-new picture of what's possible.

Habakkuk 2:2 (ESV) says to, *"Write the vision; make it plain on tablets, so he may run who reads it."* When we write a vision and keep it before our eyes, it starts to renew our mindset about what's possible. Romans 12:2 shows us that we can't live like the world, with the wrong thoughts, and expect to walk in God's will.

> *Do not conform to the pattern of this world, but be transformed by the renewing of your mind. Then you will be able to test and approve what God's will is—his good, pleasing and perfect will.*
> —Romans 12:2

So we must renew our minds, and that's what you've been doing through your Daily Faith Boosters and through the action steps in these past days. I wanted to give you a 30-day, step-by-step plan to reclaim your faith, your vision, and your health. Change always requires a plan. Having no plan is still a plan—it's just a plan to fail.

The Holy Spirit gave me a plan of action during my fast. He showed me that I needed to change my picture of possibility with the Word of God, and to do that, it was going to require me to put in some time and work. It wasn't going to happen instantly.

You see, to receive anything from God requires faith, and faith requires a renewed mind. Faith is unwavering belief in God and His promises to us. We can't just decide to be in faith or make ourselves believe. Faith is not mental assent. It is a concrete thing, not an abstract thing. It is evidence. It is substance. And building it requires us to change what we are looking at. It changes our picture of possibility. So how do we get faith?

How to Build Faith

> *Consequently, faith comes from hearing the message, and the message is heard through the word about Christ.*
>
> —Romans 10:17

First of all, when we hear the Word of God, a seed of faith is planted in our hearts. (This is why we went through the last few days of preparing the soil of our hearts and pulling out roots and rocks.) The Word is the seed. We must continue to guard that seed, water it, and nurture it to maturity, as Jesus talked about in the parable of the sower.

During my own 30-day Healing Dare, I constantly bombarded my day with the Bible. Here's a reminder of some of the things the Holy Spirit had me do:

1. Shut off all of the negative messages. This means no reading material, social media, news, radio, or television UNLESS it is teaching from the Word of God.

2. Write down as many Scriptures as you can find about healing and faith.

3. Speak those Scriptures out loud, putting them into first person, three-to-four times per day.

4. Craft a "Declaration of Faith" about your body, and speak that three-to-four times per day, along with your Scriptures.

5. Continually have preaching about healing, healing Scripture recordings, or worship music playing in your house and car.

6. Get to every church service you can to keep yourself in an atmosphere of anointing. *(Side note: My church believes in healing for all and teaches that. If your church does not, I suggest you find a new church or at least listen to teaching on healing throughout the week. What you are taught makes a huge difference when you come up against a battle. I attended all three weekend church services and then listened to the message on repeat all week long.)*

7. Put up photos and images of you being active and healthy, as well as Scriptures on healing, so you can see those all the time. Some call this a "Vision Board." Pictures are powerful tools for our brains.

Proverbs 4:20-23 say how important it is to continually meditate on God's Word:

> *My son, pay attention to what I say; turn your ear to my words. Do not let them out of your sight, keep them within your heart; for they are life to those who find them and health to one's whole body. Above all else, guard your heart, for everything you do flows from it.*

I'm ready for you to experience the same victory, faith, and power that I experienced in my own life. What God did for me, He will do for you!

Don't get discouraged if you don't feel anything changing. Just keep lifting those spiritual weights to build those faith muscles, speaking the Word of God, and doing the things listed above. God may lead you to add or subtract things based on your personal situation.

The main thing is to inundate and saturate your heart with pictures of possibility! Slowly but surely, you are getting stronger. Just like a seed that starts growing underground where no one can see it, your faith is growing and soon will bring change that all the world can see!

CAN YOU PICTURE YOURSELF HEALED?

 **READ**

Take time to write out and speak James 1:5-6:

 DETOX:

Have you let go of vision in any area of your life? Explain. How are you doing with your Daily Faith Boosters and the steps to detox your life from negative thoughts and messages? Are there still things you need to eliminate?

 SELF-REFLECTION:

How is your own 30-day Healing Dare beginning to repaint your picture of possibility?

TODAY'S TAKEAWAY:

I need to make the necessary changes that help me picture myself totally healed. And in doing so, I will receive God's vision for my life today.

PRAYER

Lord, I am so ready for change. I thank You that You are the God of the breakthrough and that You help me to have a breakthrough as I meditate on the possibilities and promises You gave me. I love You and I trust You.

REPAINT YOUR PICTURE

CREATING YOUR DECLARATION PART ONE

DAY 11

Did you know that Jesus always spoke life, even in terrible situations that looked like certain death? That's because the picture of what He saw on the inside was different than what He saw with His natural eyes. He was able to look squarely in the eyes of FACTS and speak the TRUTH He knew in His spirit.

You see, there is often a HUGE difference between the reality in the natural realm versus the potential in the spiritual realm. That's why Jesus always looked at everything in the natural realm through the eyes of faith.

Here are just a few examples of when Jesus spoke and acted out of a different reality than the natural one most people see. *(And He often said things that made His disciples go, "Huh?!")*

Fact/Natural Realm: **Their boat was sinking, and they were about to drown.**

Jesus and the disciples were crossing the Lake of Galilee when a terrible storm arose that frightened even these seasoned fishermen. It says in Luke 8:24a (NKJV), *"And they came to Him and awoke Him, saying, 'Master, Master, we are perishing!'"*

Truth/Supernatural Realm: **Jesus wasn't about to let a storm stop Him on His mission.**

He was not having it—not just the storm but the disciples' lack of faith. As soon as He spoke to the storm, it stopped; and He rebuked the disciples as if they were children afraid of getting in the bathtub: *"No big deal, guys!"*

It says in Luke 8:24b-25a (NKJV):

> *Then He arose and rebuked the wind and the raging of the water. And they ceased, and there was a calm. But He said to them, "Where is your faith?"*

Now remember, these guys were competent seamen and probably grew up in boats on the lake. This wasn't a normal storm. But Jesus looked at the situation through the eyes of faith, and He knew His assignment. He spoke Truth, and the storm immediately ran and hid in terror.

Fact/Natural Realm: Jairus's 12-year-old daughter had died while he had run to Jesus for help.

A servant was sent to tell Jairus the crushing news:

> *While He was still speaking, someone came from the ruler of the synagogue's house, saying to him, "Your daughter is dead. Do not trouble the Teacher."*
>
> —Luke 8:49 (NKJV)

Truth/Supernatural Realm: Jesus saw a different picture, and He only spoke based on that picture.

> *But when Jesus heard it, He answered him, saying, "Do not be afraid; only believe, and she will be made well." When He came into the house, He permitted no one to go in except Peter, James, and John, and the father and mother of the girl. Now all wept and mourned for her; but He said, "Do not weep; she is not dead, but sleeping." And they ridiculed Him, knowing that she*

137

was dead. But He put them all outside, took her by the hand and called, saying, "Little girl, arise." Then her spirit returned, and she arose immediately. And He commanded that she be given something to eat. And her parents were astonished, but He charged them to tell no one what had happened.

—Luke 8:50-56 (NKJV)

Notice how Jesus put out the people who were coming into agreement with death? He would only entertain the reality that she was coming back. He never even acknowledged that she was "dead," only that she was "sleeping." In other words, this was a very temporary situation.

The facts you've been presented with by doctors or that are manifesting as symptoms in your body are temporary as well! When you start to see situations the way God sees them, you realize any setback is just a setup for victory and resurrection. You realize that no matter what gets in your way on your journey, nothing can hinder your destiny when you see the future through the eyes of faith. Jesus knew He was going to the cross, and nothing, not even hurricane force winds, would take Him out before His time. You can stand on the same thing: Nothing is permitted to take you out of this race until you have completed your assignment on Earth.

Let's look at one more story to see how Jesus dealt with natural facts and brought them into alignment with spiritual Truth.

Fact/Natural Realm: Jesus's friend Lazarus had died.

In John 11, we read that the terrible news reached Jesus and His disciples. Lazarus was a close friend and supporter of the ministry. But Jesus did not see Lazarus being laid in a tomb with no breath in him as a permanent reality.

Truth/Supernatural Realm: When Jesus heard about Lazarus's death, He spoke confidently that Lazarus would live again, no question.

> *When he heard this, Jesus said, "This sickness will not end in death...." After he had said this, he went on to tell them, "Our friend Lazarus has fallen asleep; but I am going there to wake him up."*
>
> —John 11:4a, 11

His disciples tried to stop Him from getting near Jerusalem, but they finally relented, and Thomas said, "*Let us also go, that we may die with him*" (John 11:16b). What men of faith and power! Haha!

But again, Jesus was undeterred. His mission propelled Him, and His inner picture of victory said that Lazarus would rise. When He showed up at the house, Lazarus's sisters, Mary and Martha, were there mourning. Jesus spoke to Martha.

> *Jesus said to her, "Your brother will rise again." Martha answered, "I know he will rise again in the resurrection at the last day." Jesus said to her, "I am the resurrection and the life. The one who believes in me will live, even though they die; and whoever lives by believing in me will never die. Do you believe this?"*
>
> —John 11:23-26

Despite seeing the mourners and the family He loved in such deep grief, Jesus kept the picture of victory inside. The story gets pretty shocking:

> *Jesus, once more deeply moved, came to the tomb. It was a cave with a stone laid across the entrance. "Take away the stone," he said.*
>
> *"But, Lord," said Martha, the sister of the dead man, "by this time there is a bad odor, for he has been there four days."*
>
> *Then Jesus said, "**__Did I not tell you that if you believe, you will see the glory of God?__**"*
>
> *So they took away the stone. Then Jesus looked up and said, "Father, I thank you that you have heard me. I knew that you always hear me, but I said this for the benefit of the people standing here, that they may believe that you sent me."*
>
> *When he had said this, Jesus called in a loud voice, "**__Lazarus, come out!__**" The dead man came out, his hands and feet wrapped with strips of linen, and a cloth around his face.*
>
> *Jesus said to them, "**__Take off the grave clothes and let him go.__**"*
> —John 11:38-44

Jesus brought natural facts into alignment with spiritual Truth by speaking out of His inner picture of victory. **If something didn't fit in that picture of victory, He simply changed it.**

His friend dying did not fit in the picture, so He raised him from the dead!

Jesus altered the weather, cured broken bodies, brought opposing forces into submission, conquered the hardest of sinners' hearts, and cursed darkness.

Notice that Jesus always:

- Knew why He was here and where He was going.
- Lived out of His inner picture of victory.
- Spoke life to cause change.

Today, YOU are going to start writing your own picture of victory as your "Confession of Faith."

When you start speaking the Truth over the facts, things change!

Matthew 19:26 again and meditate on what it means for your problems.

DETOX:

What natural circumstances have you accepted as final? Ask the Lord to show you what HE wants to do in those situations or areas of your life.

SELF-REFLECTION:

What specific circumstance do you want to apply your faith toward changing?

What does the Bible say about that problem? If it's sickness, write your favorite healing Scripture here, but make it about YOU/put it in first person.

Now, state the change you need, but as if it has *already* happened. For instance, don't say, "My thyroid needs to start working again." Say; "My thyroid works perfectly and produces the correct hormones needed."

Journal your picture of victory over that evil circumstance.

 # TODAY'S TAKEAWAY:

I will repaint my picture with the Word daily so that faith grows in my heart.

PRAYER

Lord, I thank You that (insert your picture of victory here), because of Your power that is at work in my life. I see victory and nothing else. I reject all circumstances that are trying to come against the perfect plan You have for me. I ask You for renewed vision, in Jesus's name.

Day
12

REPAINT YOUR PICTURE

CREATING YOUR DECLARATION PART TWO

DAY 12

T oday, let's continue crafting your picture of victory into a Declaration of Faith that you will start speaking over your life in tandem with your healing Scriptures that you've been speaking three or four times per day. (You're doing it, right? Keep at it!)

As we saw in the last devotional, Jesus spoke things that looked contrary to the facts. When the little girl had died, He said, *"Do not fear; only believe, and she will be well"* (Luke 8:50b, ESV).

He defied natural law with a GREATER law, the Law of Life.

People often ask me if it's okay to acknowledge the facts about an illness. They ask if it's okay to tell others about their symptoms or diagnosis. I would say that it's fine to *listen* to a doctor's opinion, and to share what the doctor's opinion is when you are speaking to your trusted inner circle, but don't let your words or inner picture come into *agreement* with it. For instance, you could say, "The doctor's opinion is that there is cancer present, but God's Word says I am healed."

It's fine to also pursue natural remedies and use the wisdom that God has placed in the hands of medical professionals if you feel led to do so. Science is not in contradiction to God's Word since God placed the principles of biology in the earth.

However, this earth is under a curse—one that we've been redeemed from—so the natural world is not our final Truth. Realize that medical science is not the final word over your future. No matter what facts are thrown at you, you DO NOT have to accept them as your truth. Only God's Word is Truth, and only the Great Physician has the final Word!

Hannah and her husband Mark were told that they had miscarried.

Sitting in a doctor's office staring at an ultrasound screen, they saw a blood clot and an embryo with no detectable heartbeat.

Hannah was told there was nothing the doctor could do, and to take a prescription to eject the fetal tissue. Only, Mark and Hannah refused to receive that as their final Truth.

Mark said, "They are hitting it with science, but we are going to hit it with our faith."

They began speaking life over that baby, receiving prayer at church, and speaking God's Word. They got themselves into a place of perfect peace.

A week later, they went back to her doctor for another ultrasound, because they had perfect peace that the baby was still alive. The doctor was shocked to see no blood clots and a perfect baby with a heartbeat.

When she compared the scan from the prior week, she said she had never seen anything like it in all her years of practice. Mark and Hannah had a perfect baby girl!

Why? They refused to come into agreement with the death spoken by the circumstances. They came into agreement with the Life Giver, whose resurrection power was available to them and their baby.

A New Picture

Now let's look at a man who demonstrated great faith in the face of very discouraging facts. Abram was a righteous man who believed in God and lived thousands of years before Jesus was born. He and his wife, Sarai, were very old and had suffered the heartbreak of never bearing children. It was too late. Sarai was 90 years old.

But God knew the desire of their hearts, and their faith in Him caused an amazing thing to happen.

One day, Abram had a visitation from Father God, during which God started calling him something new:

> Abram fell facedown, and God said to him, "As for me, this is my covenant with you: You will be the father of many nations. No longer will you be called Abram; your name will be Abraham, for I have made you a father of many nations. I will make you very fruitful; I will make nations of you, and kings will come from you. I will establish my covenant as an everlasting covenant between me and you and your descendants after you for the generations to come, to be your God and the God of your descendants after you."
>
> —Genesis 17:3-7

The name "Abram" means "multitude," but God wanted Abram's name to become a faith statement, to paint a new picture of victory, so He changed his name to "Abraham."

In the Hebrew, Abraham means father of many. How strange to call a childless man "father of many," right?

But God knows there is power in what we call ourselves.

Now, every time someone would call Abraham's name, they would be prophesying his future and reminding him of what God promised.

God also changed Sarai's name, which in Hebrew had more of a masculine quality, to "Sarah," which means "princess of a multitude" and has more feminine qualities.

Sure enough, miraculously, Isaac was born to Abraham and Sarah.

In this next passage, still talking about Abraham, we find a key insight to God's mode of operation and the spiritual law we enact when we are in faith.

> *Therefore, the promise comes by faith, so that it may be by grace and may be guaranteed to all Abraham's offspring—not only to those who are of the law but also to those who have the faith of Abraham. He is the father of us all. As it is written: "I have made you a father of many nations." He is our father in the sight of God, in whom he believed—**the God who gives life to the dead and calls into being things that were not**.*
>
> —Romans 4:16-17

God calls into being things that weren't there a moment ago! That's what He did when He spoke and the world came into existence. *"And God said, 'Let there be light,' and there was light"* (Genesis 1:3). He doesn't look at a dark universe and let that darkness remain. He speaks, and there is light! He doesn't look at that sick body you've been carrying around and leave you in hopelessness. He sent forth *the Word*, His Son Jesus, to heal you (Psalm 107:20, John 1:1-5).

God wanted to repaint Abraham's picture, so He changed his name.

Every time Abraham introduced himself, he was saying, "Hello! My name is Father of Multitudes!" God was able to bring life to Sarah's womb because Abraham believed the promise of God and spoke it.

> *Against all hope, Abraham in hope believed and so became the father of many nations, just as it had been said to him, "So shall your offspring be." Without weakening in his faith, **he faced the fact** that his body was as good as dead—since he was about a hundred years old—and that Sarah's womb was also dead. Yet **he did not waver** through unbelief regarding the promise of God, but was strengthened in his faith and gave glory to God, **being fully persuaded that God had power to do what he had promised**.*
>
> —Romans 4:18-21

What is faith? That's the picture of it right there.

Faith is being fully persuaded, fully convinced, and not wavering in unbelief.

Notice that Abraham faced the facts and yet still believed the mightier Truth of God's promise to him. And that's what we are to do too.

Be Fully Persuaded

How do we get "in faith" or become fully persuaded that God's promises are true?

Faith comes through hearing the Word through our spiritual ears. *"So then faith comes by hearing, and hearing by the word of God"* (Romans 10:17, NKJV). That's why you need to keep up with your Daily Faith Boosters!

Believing comes from hearing the Truth, and the only way we can hear the Truth in our spirits is by listening to the Word of God. Truth is revealed to our spirits when we read and speak Scripture. Each Scripture is God-breathed, active, and powerful to bring change to our inner pictures. You can't make your picture change by the force of your will. It requires active power that is only found in one source—the Words of Life. Abraham received the words God spoke to him as his NEW Truth, even though reality was staring him in the face every time he looked in the mirror.

Today, finish writing your own "Confession of Faith" based on who you are in Christ and the picture of victory that He provided for you on the cross.

I want you to imagine total and final victory over whatever sickness or circumstance you are facing.

Do you see it in your spirit?

Now, write that as a statement that is ALREADY REALITY. Include what you wrote yesterday and add to it. For example:

> "I was healed of scoliosis, and I can walk, run, and live my life with strength, flexibility, and with no pain! I am completing my mission to be a godly wife and successful entrepreneur who funds the Kingdom of God. I am God's child, and nothing can stand in my way. Fear has no place in me. Death

THE 30-DAY HEALING DARE

has no place in me. Sickness has no place in me! According to Romans 8:11, if the Spirit of Him who raised Jesus from the dead is living in me, He who raised Christ from the dead will also give life to my mortal body because of His Spirit who lives in me!"

Now, add one more thing. Add a sentence *commanding* the circumstance to go, in the name of Jesus. For instance:

"Scoliosis, leave now and never return! Body, come into alignment with the Word of God! Pain, you are defeated and you must go now! I curse this illness and command it to wither at the roots."

You can reference my Confession of Faith that I spoke daily, located in the appendix of this book. Then, finish writing and finalizing your own, either below or in your own journal.

MY CONFESSION OF FAITH:

 **READ**

Hebrews 4:12

 ## DETOX:

Are there things in your house that speak of sickness? Remind you of the problem? Try to get rid of them, or at least move them out of sight. Let your eyes only see victory wherever they look.

 ## SELF-REFLECTION:

Put on some worship music and do what I call a "prayer march." Take your Confession of Faith in your hand, march around your room, and declare it out loud. Do it over and over until you feel God's power start to rise up on the inside of you. Then just praise God for the victory! When we reflect on God's greatness through worship, plus speak His Word, our spirits get so much stronger.

 ## TODAY'S TAKEAWAY:

I speak life to my body and health to my bones. I will be mindful of my words because they carry power to bless or curse.

PRAYER

Jesus, thank You for helping me to see possibilities instead of problems, to see promise instead of pain, to see miracles instead of this mess. I receive Your picture of victory in my spirit, in Your mighty name! I rebuke the spirits of doubt and fear right now, and I say they have no place in me. I do not have a spirit of unbelief but unshakable faith!

REPAINT YOUR PICTURE

ACTIVATING YOUR WORDS

DAY 13

Y ou're almost halfway through The *30-day Healing Dare*, and I'm so excited about this next part!

We had to first lay the foundation and get the "bad stuff" out, but now it's time to focus on planting the good stuff! How do you do that? *Through your words.*

Remember what Jesus did when He came up against a circumstance that needed to change? He:

- Knew why He was here and where He was going. (identity/purpose).
- Lived out of His inner picture of victory. (faith/being fully persuaded).
- Spoke life to cause change. (released power through words).

When you come up against scary or difficult circumstances, you must do the same. Don't take it lying down! Remind yourself of who you are, focus on the picture of victory found in the Bible, and speak life to that circumstance.

Like children, we must get excited about the possibilities God has given us. For instance, my kids get excited when I tell them I just ordered them a new toy they've been wanting. They are fully persuaded that I will keep my word.

What happens when I tell them something good is on the way? How do my kids talk? They immediately start asking, "When will it arrive?! I want to play with it! It's gonna be so cool! I'm so excited! Thank you, Mommy!"

Next, they wait at the door for the delivery to come, fully expecting that every time the doorbell rings, it's their new toy. They tell others about it. They anticipate what it will be like to play with it. They talk as if they already have it! Why?

They are convinced that I am telling the truth, even though they don't yet have it in their hands.

The words coming out of their mouths are not words of doubt and unbelief. My six-year-old doesn't tell his friends, "Well, Mom said she ordered me a toy, but I doubt it. I don't think I'll ever have it. It's probably not her will to give it to me." Yet that's exactly how we talk about the promises of God.

If our hearts are not fully persuaded, we tend to talk words of doubt and unbelief. We don't get excited about what God promised, because we don't believe He meant what He said.

Just like kids, when we are actually convinced that something amazing has been given to us, we talk about it. Our words line up with the reality of what is ours. Whatever the heart believes is what the mouth is going to speak (Luke 6:45). Paul, the apostle said it this way:

> *"It is written: 'I believed; therefore I have spoken.' Since we have that same spirit of faith, we also believe and therefore speak, because we know that the one who raised the Lord Jesus from the dead will also raise us with Jesus and present us with you to himself."*
>
> —2 Corinthians 4:13-14

THE 30-DAY HEALING DARE

When we believe, our words reflect our belief.

So now, let me ask you, if I eavesdropped on you today, would I hear words of death, doubt, despair, and discouragement? Or would I hear words of possibility, promise, and persuasion that God's Word is ALREADY Truth in your life?

Take It Seriously

Jesus took words very seriously. He spoke this rebuke to the Pharisees, who were religious folks but lacked a real relationship with God:

> "A good man brings good things out of the good stored up in him, and an evil man brings evil things out of the evil stored up in him. But I tell you that everyone will have to give account on the day of judgment <u>for every empty word they have spoken. For by your words you will be acquitted, and by your words you will be condemned.</u>"
>
> —Matthew 12:35-37

People get all bent out of shape when we talk about speaking by faith, and label it "name it, claim it nonsense," but it's not a human idea or doctrine of men. You can argue against it all you want, but it's God's law. It's His idea.

How do I know? Jesus demonstrated it and then told us to do it, as illustrated in the following story.

One day, Jesus was walking with His disciples, and they came upon a fig tree. He unexpectedly cursed the fig tree, saying, "*May no one ever eat fruit from you again*" (Mark 11:14b). His disciples heard Him, which is what Jesus intended. He was trying to teach them about this principle of words. They probably thought, "Okay, that was really weird!" But the next morning, they passed by the same fig tree, and it was brown, dry, and DEAD. It withered up from the roots in 24 hours! The disciples were very shocked and questioned Jesus about how He did that. His reply was:

> *"Have faith in God," Jesus answered. "Truly I tell you, if anyone **says** to this mountain, 'Go, throw yourself into the sea,' and does not doubt in their heart but believes that what they say will happen, it will be done for them. Therefore I tell you, whatever you **ask for** in prayer, believe that you **have** received it, and it will be yours. And when you stand praying, if you hold anything against anyone, forgive them, so that your Father in heaven may forgive you your sins."*
>
> —Mark 11:22-26

Notice the references to speaking in this Scripture? When I was going through my 30-day Healing Dare, the Holy Spirit pointed out this Scripture and specifically told me to curse the growth in my abdomen and command it to wither and die at the roots.

I found out later that tumors and growths steal nourishment from the bloodstream, and I believe when I started cursing that thing in my stomach, its supply of nourishment was instantly cut off. However, it took about a month for me to see the total transformation. Notice in this Scripture Jesus said, *"Believe that you HAVE received it, and it WILL be yours."* Just like that child whose parent told them a toy was on its way, we need to believe our Father God when He says we HAVE received it (by faith), and it WILL be ours. One is past tense, and one is future tense, but we must live, speak, and act in the past tense FINISHED and COMPLETED work of Christ that paid for our healing. Then we must SPEAK!

To further illustrate this principle of asking and receiving, let me tell you what just happened to me. I was out shopping for gifts, and I saw a very cute coat hanging in my favorite store, Altar'd State. I looked at it, looked at the price tag, and decided I had better focus on getting the kids' gifts for Christmas. But before I walked away, I said to the Lord, "God, I really love that coat. I'd love that one. Thank you, Lord!"

Now, let me preface this by saying I'm constantly giving away clothing to others, so I knew I had "seed in the ground" and a "harvest" coming. (If you don't know what I mean by those terms, it's a principle Jesus talked about called sowing and reaping. It works just like sowing seeds and reaping a harvest on the earth. For more on this topic, you need to read the book, *Your Financial Revolution: The Power of Provision* by my dad, Gary Keesee.)

I don't ask God for many material things, but I really liked that coat! I didn't tell a soul about it and forgot about it. That is until several weeks later when I opened a gift from my executive assistant. There inside the box was the very coat I had prayed about! I immediately called my assistant to tell her! Why did that coat come? Because I had given away some of that same thing to others, so I had seed in the ground. Then I used my words to speak my petition to God when I said, "I'll take that one!" My words brought that coat. (And my assistant followed the leading of the Holy Spirit!)

When our faith can see victory, and our minds are agreeing with God's picture, it's time to speak some things into existence! Just like God spoke and created, we can speak and create. Jesus said to use our words to bring our inner picture of victory into existence in the natural realm, despite what we see with our natural eyes. He also said, *"Ask, and the gift is yours. Seek, and you'll discover. Knock, and the door will be opened for you"* (Matthew 7:7, TPT).

Here are a few more Scriptures about the power of our words:

> *Death and life are in the power of the tongue, and those who love it will eat its fruits.*
>
> —Proverbs 18:21 (ESV)

> *So shall my word be that goes out from my mouth; it shall not return to me empty, but it shall accomplish that which I purpose, and shall succeed in the thing for which I sent it.*
>
> —Isaiah 55:11 (ESV)

> *Gracious words are like a honeycomb, sweetness to the soul and health to the body.*
>
> —Proverbs 16:24 (ESV)

Our words are powerful when they align with His will to heal us. Healing came along with the "benefits package" of salvation! And we receive healing just like we receive salvation, by believing and speaking.

> *Because, if you **confess with your mouth** that Jesus is Lord and **believe in your heart** that God raised him from the dead, you will be saved.*
>
> —Romans 10:9 (ESV)

Today, focus on speaking your picture of victory over your life, just like Jesus did. **STOP letting life happen to you, and START speaking life to what is happening!**

As you read your Daily Faith Booster Scriptures, imagine the picture inside of your heart being repainted as each brushstroke from the Word of God completes the image of total victory. Then, speak out your Confession of Faith you wrote yesterday, and believe that it is causing change in your physical circumstances.

Speaking life brings change to your inner picture of possibility.

 **READ**

Psalm 34:12-13

 **DETOX:**

What words do you need to eliminate from your vocabulary? Ask the Holy Spirit to show you.

SELF-REFLECTION:

Have you been owning the problem by saying, "My_____ (insert problem here)"? Start owning the promise instead by saying, "My _____ (insert what you're receiving from God by faith)."

TODAY'S TAKEAWAY:

My tongue is the rudder of my life, so I will steer it with words of faith and clarity.

PRAYER

Thank You, Jesus for my healing that You already paid for! I take it by faith, and I thank You that it's mine, just like salvation is mine. I already have it! Thank You that every symptom is gone from my body NOW. In Your name, I pray."

REPAINT YOUR PICTURE

BELIEVING THE IMPOSSIBLE

DAY 14

God is in the healing business, and He LOVES doing the things we would call impossible. It makes His heart happy to show His power on our behalves! But we must invite His power in our lives through our belief in Him. Amanda did just that when she was facing a painful medical condition. Here's the testimony she sent me:

> Hi, Pastor Amy! I wanted to let you know I was healed at the service where you preached on healing! I had been diagnosed with GERD after a scope that showed damage to my esophagus and stomach. I was put on a medication that cost $230 per month. I also had to cut out every potentially triggering food, have my bed raised at the head, sleep on a $300 incline pillow, and take all kinds of supplements—and nothing worked.
>
> I felt like I was choking all of the time for two years. Those GERD drugs are nasty! They cause all kinds of problems, especially in women, from osteoporosis to lupus!
>
> Anyway, during your sermon, you instructed us to lay hands on each other for healing, and I laid hands on myself. From that moment, I was completely healed and have never had another symptom. I drink coffee, eat spicy food and everything else freely. I never took another pill, and I never will!
>
> Thank you for your testimony and healing anointing.
>
> That weekend, we had also invited a friend whose 11-year-old son was stricken with blindness from some rare disease. Their son's condition was remarkably improved! She and her husband have been going to Faith Life Church ever since.
>
> —Amanda

Amanda is a vibrant part of our church body today, and she serves in various ministries. She is a great example of someone who took God's Word at face value, despite the pain she was in.

If you are dealing with physical symptoms in your body, it can feel like a huge mountain. But Jesus said we can see that mountain move when we believe and speak to it. Nothing is impossible with God (Luke 1:37).

Another translation of that verse says, "*For the Word of God will never fail*" (NLT). The Word doesn't fail. God doesn't lie. His promises to you are as certain as the sunrise!

Hebrews 3:6 (NLT) says, "*But Christ, as the Son, is in charge of God's entire house. And we are God's house, if we keep our courage and remain confident in our hope in Christ.*"

Our Fuzzy Filter

Since we've grown up in this cursed earth, filled with fear, we have been programmed from a young age to see things through a lens of fear and impossibilities. We have studied the effects of the curse all our lives. Thus, it's hard for us to trust what we cannot confirm with our five senses or what doesn't line up with that filter of the curse.

We analyze situations through messages and input we receive on a daily basis. For instance, we are told or have seen that cancer kills people, so the first thing we think when we hear the word *cancer* is death. We have taken in fear-based messages through media, music, people's words, and even through what we learned in school. That's why those in the medical field often have a harder time receiving healing by faith. They have had to spend their career studying what could go wrong. They study the effects of the earth curse every day. That has become their filter. It often takes doctors and nurses longer to repaint their inner pictures because they have more known worst-case scenarios in their brains to overcome. They have seen many cases that ended in death. They have a lot of mental pictures that are hard to process.

My friend, who is a nurse, went in for a routine ultrasound during one of her pregnancies. She saw what the doctor saw: swelling in the baby's brain. She knew what that meant. She was trained in the medical field to look for the problems. But she also had heard enough stories of healing and she had heard the Word of God long enough to know that all things are possible.

She and her husband left there declaring that their baby would live and not die. They spoke life. They refused to come into agreement with the bad report. Even though she was a nurse who knew all of the natural implications, she leaned to what her spirit was saying. And her spirit diagnosed this situation as POSSIBLE! Instead of seeing death, she and her husband spoke life.

They had another ultrasound weeks later. And there on the scan, in stark contrast to their previous scan, they saw that the swelling on the baby's brain was completely gone!

Despite what she knew from her natural training, this nurse had spiritual training! She knew she had to overcome the temptation to walk in fear. She had to lean to her greater nature—the nature of God inside of her. And she did! Her baby was born completely normal and healthy.

Sometimes we need to unlearn a lot of things in order to receive from God. That's why Jesus said we need to become like little children. We need to get our minds to the point of innocence, almost naivety, so that we can believe a Higher Authority. If we can become naive to what the world says could go wrong, and become knowledgeable of what the Bible says could go right, I think most of our problems would be reversed.

Innocence is not ignorance. It's trust. It's purity of heart. When the Word is our filter, it cleans our heart of impurity and repaints a picture of possibility. It speaks of a greater future outcome than what the earth curse says is possible.

In God's Strength, Not Yours

God spoke the following word of encouragement to me a few years ago during a trying time when it seemed things just weren't changing in my life:

> "How" is not a problem you need to solve, because there's a solution waiting to happen if you'll have faith. And it is My job to make it happen through you. If you will simply follow My step-by-step instructions and soak your mind in the Word so you do not allow the cares of life to choke out your faith, all things shall be possible for you. In this last hour, I look for sons and daughters who are ruminating in the Word, who are soaking their souls in the Word, who are meditating day and night on what I say. Stop looking at what the world says.
>
> Those who listen to what I say will have what I have. Those

who do what Jesus did will have what I have. Those who step out in faith will have the fruit of faith. Those who walk in my ways will see good days.

Stop thinking about the how—stop worrying and "problem-solving." You are to be solution minded, not problem minded. Stop looking at the lack of "how" as being a problem. Do you not think that I know the how?! Do you not think that I know how everything works?! I formed every mitochondria and cell in the world. I breathed the atoms and the molecules into existence. I fused the table of elements. The energy in my voice literally created balls of energy that you call stars. And then I named all the stars just for fun. I created so many animals that you cannot name them all, and you cannot know them all. But each and every one is different and brings me glory in a different way.

How I long to see creation renewed. How I long to see my children walking in the fruit of faith in Me. If you will take the ceiling off of your life and realize that all things are possible, then fear will bounce off of you like rain off of a windshield. You will see it on the outside, but it will not touch you or get you wet.

That word from the Lord set me on a new path in my thinking. I was freed from "figuring everything out."

In the next day's devotion, I'm going to share how God totally and suddenly changed everything during that trying season of my life when I had to get my attention back on Him and come into agreement with His promises.

Maybe it's a firstborn tendency, but it's easy for me to try to do things in my own strength. I tell myself, *"I'm strong. I can do it. I'll just work harder. I'll bear more responsibility."* But the things God wants to have happen in our lives cannot be done in the flesh. They are too big! They are too great! We must walk by the spirit.

We talked previously on another day about Abraham and Sarah's miracle child, but I didn't tell you the whole story.

Abraham first tried to fulfill things in the flesh, through his carnal thinking, and things didn't turn out great. He made the mistake of trying to make the promise of God happen in his own power. Here's what happened.

Sarah suggested that Abraham take her servant, Hagar, as his other wife in hopes of having a child. They were desperate, and this was a shortcut it seemed. So that's what Abraham did. And sure enough, Hagar had a son they named Ishmael.

> *The Scriptures say that Abraham had two sons, one from his slave wife and one from his freeborn wife. The son of the slave wife was born in a human attempt to bring about the fulfillment of God's promise. But the son of the freeborn wife was born as God's own fulfillment of his promise.*
>
> —Galatians 4:22-23 (NLT)

Conflicts arose in Abraham's family, as you can imagine. As he became a teenager, Ishmael even tried to kill Isaac, the son born of the promise. Abraham had to eventually send Ishmael and Hagar away.

With Abraham's human attempt at fulfilling the promise, there was sorrow. It wasn't God's way. But when God brings a blessing, there is no sorrow attached (Proverbs 10:22).

Today, stop trying to focus on HOW God is going to do something. Relinquish your worry. Surrender false responsibility. Don't try to pursue something in your own strength. Trust and know that you serve the God of the impossible, and He has made a way where there seems to be no way. Rest in His peace. If you struggle with over-analyzing things and worrying about the "how," know that God is trustworthy and faithful. Trust and believe.

Read Romans 8:5-11, which talks about doing things in the spirit versus the flesh.

Write down three worries that you have not given to God and perhaps have been trying to fix in your own strength. Small or large, God cares about them.

1.

2.

3.

SELF-REFLECTION:

Take the concerns you listed and write a note to God, relinquish control, and give Him those cares. He is able!

 # TODAY'S TAKEAWAY:

I will not live my life through the lens of the earth curse, but I will see through the eyes of faith to repaint my picture.

 ## PRAYER

Jesus, I receive Your "how" for my problem. Lead me to the right actions and help me not to make things happen in myself. I receive Your power for every situation. I give You control. I refocus on Your faithfulness in my life.

REPAINT YOUR PICTURE

BELIEVING IS SEEING

A t the end of our last devotion, I shared a word I received from God during a trying period in my life. Now, let me tell you what happened during that season Jason and I found ourselves in. I think it illustrates well how we can try things in our own strength or we can lean to our spirits.

We were living in a small rental house that did not feel like home, with two small children, and we were actively looking for a house to buy. Everything that went on the market was selling in just a day or two. We just couldn't seem to find the right house. We had our needs provided, but we weren't walking in the promise.

During this time, we also experienced some challenges, betrayals, and setbacks that required a lot of time, attention, and emotional strength. I felt like we were in the wilderness. I was stressed out, and nothing seemed to be going well. That was when God gave me that word of encouragement that I shared in the last devotion.

We must have looked at over 15 houses in person and a 100 or more houses online. Nothing that we looked at was close to what we sowed for. We started to get very frustrated. Important note: the enemy wants to get you frustrated so you step out of faith. If you are frustrated, you come out of agreement with God's Word, and it's a sign you're not trusting God that you already have the answer. You aren't able to receive from someone you don't trust. It thus prevents God's promise from happening.

One night, Jason said to me, "Hey, let's take a break. We are looking at house after house, and nothing is coming close. We already sowed a seed for this house, so we have it; and God will direct our steps when it's time." At that moment, with tears streaming down my face,

I told God, "Okay, I give you these problems. I'm going to stop trying to figure this out. We are too busy to struggle with finding a house, so you're going to have to show us where it is at the right time. We are done searching in our own strength. We are going to stay faithful to our assignment and trust you to bring the house. Please make sure we don't miss it."

We quit looking at the real estate sites. We took a break from the search. That sounds foolish, but we were done trying in our own strength. Peace came into our hearts. I stopped stressing out.

Several months later, we pulled into the driveway of the rental house, and my daughter, who was only five years old at the time, said, "Mom, it's time to move."

"What did you say?" I asked.

"It's time to move to the big white house with the stairs that go up to my bedroom," she replied confidently.

I didn't know what on earth she was talking about, but she had my attention.

"Did you have a dream about a house?" I asked her.

She gave me a quick, "Yes," as she hopped out of the car.

After I got the kids to bed, I talked to Jason about what our daughter had said. I thought it was very unusual. "Maybe that's a sign you should look online tonight," he said. I immediately grabbed my phone and started searching the real estate app for the first time in months. Two houses popped up that matched our search criteria. One was a bit cheaper, but it was smaller, and it wasn't everything we wanted. The other was a white two-story with a spiral staircase on 10 beautiful park-like acres, with a pond and seclusion. Both had just come on the market a few days ago. Both needed some rehab.

I called our realtor right then and told her we had two houses we wanted to look at. She said, "The only time I can show you those properties is 9:00 a.m. tomorrow morning because I'm going out of town." We agreed to meet her there bright and early.

The next morning, she called and said, "I'm sorry, but the smaller house just went into contract. I can show you the bigger white house though."

When we pulled up in the driveway, we knew it was the one. We felt such peace hit both of us that we barely needed to look at the inside. This was it!

Now, I have to confess, I like fixer uppers, but Jason had been against doing a renovation. However, when he saw this house, which was an "as-is" foreclosure Fannie Mae property, he had no objections. He had peace, despite ALL the work that needed done (and it was a lot!) I knew then it *had* to be God! Haha!

The realtor called the selling agent, and when she got off the phone, she said, "Well, unfortunately, the selling realtor says it's already in contract."

My husband is tenacious, and he wasn't giving up. "It says here that it's still on the market," he said. "Can we just try submitting an of-fer?" She said that, yes, it was allowing her to submit an offer. We did so that same day. Long story short, there were multiple offers on the table by the end of that same day, and within a few days, the bank had decided to accept our offer, even though we only offered asking price! (We found out later that the selling agent didn't want us to submit an offer and had lied because she had a client that would have given her double commission as the seller's AND the buyer's agent.)

When we got the call that we were the chosen offer, we were ecstatic! This property ticked all the boxes on our list! It had a huge wrap-around porch just like I always wanted. It had mature trees and a gorgeous pond. The only thing that DID NOT line up with our list of wants was the price—it was $20,000 over what we had written down on our petition to God. Jason had felt to offer asking price though, and we had peace about it.

Now, here's the really awesome part of this story: The inspection obviously showed that the house needed work. It also showed that the roof needed replaced within the next few years. My husband had an idea based on that note from the inspector. He called a roofer to get an estimate on a new roof, and it came back at $20,000. It's a big roof because of that wraparound porch! Jason felt to ask the bank for a concession of $20,000 off the asking price of the house based on that roof estimate. Our realtor warned us that the bank could back out and go with another buyer if we tried asking for too much. She also reminded us that this was an "as-is" property and that she had never seen this large of a concession for a foreclosure property in her 25 years as a realtor.

However, Jason and I had a strong urgency to move forward. We wrote a letter to the bank with the request for a concession of $20,000 and prayed over it before sending it. Our realtor was shocked when the bank came back and knocked that much off the asking price of the house!

NOW the house matched every one of our requests we had asked God for. We had a picture of victory, and everything that didn't line up with that picture had to change.

After the closing came the renovations. Again, we didn't know how we were going to pay for everything that needed done. But things started happening. A business owner contacted us and said that God told him to bless us, so he bought us new windows for the front of the house and new exterior doors! Other wonderful friends and family members helped us do much of the work. Someone told us about a surplus auction where we bought supplies for one-third of the retail price. We bought $18,000 worth of beautiful kitchen cabinets for $3,800 there. Blessing after unexpected blessing flowed into our lives!

And several years after living at the house, a windstorm knocked two shingles off the roof... you know, the old roof that needed replaced anyway. The insurance company called us offering to come and check for damages from the storm, and they paid for most of the new roof. Someone else gave us $8,000, so we had a new roof for free!

The cool thing about this story is that God didn't let us miss the house. We saw it within days of it going on the market because my daughter said what she said about "the white house with the stairs." My daughter spoke up about her dream, so we did not miss what God had for us. Jason followed the leading of the Holy Spirit and did not take the word of the selling agent, so we went ahead and put in an offer. We asked for the roof concession, which brought the house into our agreed upon budget. At the time of this writing, our house is now worth two-thirds MORE than what we paid for it! God knew HOW. We just had to let Him lead us each step of the way.

Let me share my husband, Jason's, favorite Scripture with you, the one we stood on during this season:

> *Now to Him who is able to [carry out His purpose and] do superabundantly more than all that we dare ask or think [infinitely beyond our greatest prayers, hopes, or dreams], according to His power that is at work within us.*
>
> —Ephesians 3:20 (AMP)

God is able! He can do the impossibly huge things! His power is at work within us! Because Jason and I had learned how to believe and receive from God through smaller needs, we were able to have faith for this much larger need. We walked into our promise with no sorrow! Now, I didn't say *no work*. We definitely had to put in some elbow grease and diligence. But it was so worth it.

We could have tried to make things happen in our own strength (and we have made that mistake before) but it's just not as fun. It's exciting to trust the Lord and watch His faithfulness unfold in blessing after blessing, answer after answer.

Do you often worry about how to make something work? That thinking comes from the curse that came upon mankind in Genesis 3:17. But we can live in a new reality, the blessing of the Lord, as detailed in Genesis 12:1-3, Deuteronomy 28:1-14, and Psalm 91.

Forget that old adage, "If it's gonna be, it's up to me," and start saying, "With God, all things are possible!"

If you're experiencing a season of "stuck," where things just don't seem to be changing, let our testimony and the following Scripture encourage you.

 **READ**

Psalm 107:19-22:

> *Then they cried to the Lord in their trouble, and he saved them from their distress. He sent out his word and healed them; he rescued them from the grave. Let them give thanks to the Lord for his unfailing love and his wonderful deeds for mankind. Let them sacrifice thank offerings and tell of his works with songs of joy.*

 # SELF-REFLECTION:

Remind yourself of past faith victories in your life, no matter how small, and praise God for them. If you are new to this and don't yet have your own stories, find one in the Bible that shows the power of God. If He did it for one, He will do it for all who believe (Romans 2:11, Ephesians 6:9).

 # TODAY'S TAKEAWAY:

I let go of the need to make things happen in my own strength, and I trust the Holy Spirit to show me how to live this life free from the earth curse.

PRAYER

Lord God, I put my full confidence in You. I thank You that in all things, You are working for my good because I love You and I have been called according to Your purpose (Romans 8:28).

REPAINT YOUR PICTURE

A HEALTHY SPIRIT

DAY 16

A s we continue talking about building faith and repainting our picture of possibility, I think it's important to talk about our daily regimen of faith building. You already have your Daily Faith Boosters, and I hope you have been diligent with those. But let's talk more about the spirit/body connection.

Did you know that if you neglect your spiritual health, it affects your physical and mental health? We tend to separate "medical science" and spiritual faith, but they are inextricably connected. In fact, science continues to prove what we already know from the Word of God.

Hundreds of studies by renowned institutions have shown the power of weekly religious service attendance, prayer, intercession, and meditation on physical health. Let's look at some of these and plan ways you can up your spiritual health in order to repaint your picture of possibility. (Hint: you're doing one of them right now!)

Dr. Harold G. Koenig is on the faculty at Duke University as a tenured associate professor of psychiatry and an associate professor of medicine. He has spent years analyzing scientific research about faith's impact on the body and life expectancy through The Center for the Study of Religion/Spirituality and Health at Duke University. He put a large group of these studies into perspective, showing the benefits of faith:

> In three of three studies, you find a connection between religious involvement and immune and endocrine function; in five of seven studies, the religious experience lowers mortality from cancer; in 14 of 23, they have significantly lower blood pressure; in 11 of 14, they have lower mortality; and

in 12 of 13, clergy mortality is lower... Religious attendance particularly affects cardiovascular disease and stress-related diseases....[1]

In another interview, Dr. Koenig confirmed the connection between faith and health:

Studies have shown prayer can prevent people from getting sick—and when they do get sick, prayer can help them get better faster. An exhaustive analysis of more than 1,500 reputable medical studies "indicates people who are more religious and pray more have better mental and physical health," Dr. Koenig says. "And out of 125 studies that looked at the link between health and regular worship, 85 showed regular churchgoers live longer. There's a lot of evidence out there."[2]

An article entitled "Science Proves the Healing Power of Prayer" says,

Research at San Francisco General Hospital looked at the effect of prayer on 393 cardiac patients. Half were prayed for by strangers who had only the patients' names. Those patients had fewer complications, fewer cases of pneumonia, and needed less drug treatment. They also got better quicker and left the hospital earlier....

"The proof of the power of prayer is overwhelming," says researcher and writer Tom Knox, a one-time atheist who became a regular

---

[1] "Is Prayer Good for Your Health? A Critique of the Scientific Research." The Heritage Foundation. December 22, 2003. Accessed January 6, 2021. https://www.heritage.org/civil-society/report/prayer-good-your-health-critique-the-scientific-research

[2] "Science Proves the Healing Power of Prayer." Newsmax. March 31, 2015. https://www.newsmax.com/Health/Headline/prayer-health-faith-medicine/2015/03/31/id/635623

worshipper after doing an in-depth study of the medical benefits of faith.

"What I discovered astonished me," admits Knox. "Over the past 30 years, a growing and largely unnoticed body of scientific work shows religious belief is medically, socially, and psychologically beneficial."

Study after study backs up the benefits of having faith, especially in that it prolongs life. In 2006, population researchers at the University of Texas discovered that the more often you go to church, the longer you live. Concluded Knox: "Atheists can sneer at faith all they like, but they can't assume science is on their side."[3]

Another very similar study was conducted by Dr. Randolph Byrd, which had only born-again Christians praying for patients. His study discovered that the patients who received prayer needed fewer antibiotics, had less heart failure, and had less chance of developing pneumonia. He concluded that "Intercessory prayer to a Judeo-Christian God has a beneficial effect in patients admitted to a coronary care unit."[4]

You have a 29% greater survival rate if you attend church weekly, according to a McCullough meta-analysis published in 2000, while another study suggests that for women it might be as high as 52%!

That means 3,582,000 additional women might possibly be alive

---

[3] "Science Proves the Healing Power of Prayer." Newsmax. March 31, 2015. https://www.newsmax.com/Health/Headline/prayer-health-faith-medicine/2015/03/31/id/635623

[4] "Is Prayer Good for Your Health? A Critique of the Scientific Research." The Heritage Foundation. December 22, 2003. Accessed January 6, 2021. https://www.heritage.org/civil-society/report/prayer-good-your-health-critique-the-scientific-research

186

as a result of weekly church attendance, according to a Strawbridge study. [5]

So the body reacts when the spirit is kept fit and healthy through prayer and church attendance. **In the atmosphere of faith, physical cells react and come back into alignment with the Creator's intended function!**

Now, some of us have what I call a suppressed *spiritual* immune system. In the same way that someone with a weak immune system catches every virus and cold with which they come in contact, someone with a suppressed spiritual immune system has a harder time fighting off the attacks of infirmity and fear.

When our spirits are weak, undernourished, and neglected, every attack of the devil can rattle us. Just like we shouldn't wait until we're physically sick to build our immune systems, we don't want to wait until we are already sick or under attack to start a regimen of spirit building. Why play catch up when we can operate in prevention? We must build our spiritual immune systems so they are able to resist every germ and lie the enemy throws our way.

How to Build Your Spiritual Immune System
How can we build our spiritual immune systems? Here's a list of suggestions from the Bible. (Can you tell I love lists? Haha!)

---

[5] "Is Prayer Good for Your Health? A Critique of the Scientific Research." The Heritage Foundation. Dec. 22, 2003. Accessed Jan. 6, 2021. https://www.heritage.org/civil-society/report/prayer-good-your-health-critique-the-scientific-research

Attend church and pursue fellowship with other believers:

- *"And let us consider how we may spur one another on toward love and good deeds, not giving up meeting together, as some are in the habit of doing, but encouraging one another—and all the more as you see the Day approaching"* (Hebrews 10:24-25).
- *"Let the word of Christ dwell in you richly, teaching and admonishing one another in all wisdom, singing psalms and hymns and spiritual songs, with thankfulness in your hearts to God"* (Colossians 3:16, ESV).
- *"Confess your faults one to another, and pray one for another, that ye may be healed"* (James 5:16a, KJV).
- Dwight L. Moody said, "Church attendance is as vital to a disciple as a transfusion of rich, healthy blood to a sick man."

Pursue laughter and joy:

- *"Always be joyful"* (1 Thessalonians 5:16, CEV).
- *"Rejoice in the Lord always. I will say it again: Rejoice!"* (Philippians 4:4).
- *"A cheerful heart is good medicine, but a broken spirit saps a person's strength"* (Proverbs 17:22, NLT).
- *"You have turned my mourning into joyful dancing. You have taken away my clothes of mourning and clothed me with joy"* (Psalm 30:11, NLT).

Pray about everything:

- *"Never stop praying"* (1 Thessalonians 5:17, NLT).
- *"But you, dear friends, by building yourselves up in your*

most holy faith and praying in the Holy Spirit" (Jude 1:20).

- "*Keep <u>actively</u> watching and praying that you may not come into temptation; the spirit is willing, but the body is weak*" (Matthew 26:41, AMP).
- "*And pray in the Spirit on all occasions with all kinds of prayers and requests. With this in mind, be alert and always keep on praying for all the Lord's people*" (Ephesians 6:18).
- "*Is anyone among you in trouble? Let them pray*" (James 5:13a).
- "*The earnest prayer of a righteous person has great power and produces wonderful results*" (James 5:16b, NLT).
- "*But you, dear friends, must build each other up in your most holy faith, pray in the power of the Holy Spirit*" (Jude 1:20, NLT).

Spend time with Jesus and worship Him:

- "*Look to the Lord and his strength; seek his face always*" (1 Chronicles 16:11).
- "*He says, "Be still, and know that I am God; I will be exalted among the nations, I will be exalted in the earth*" (Psalm 46:10).
- "*Come near to God and he will come near to you...*" (James 4:8a).
- "*You will show me the path of life; in Your presence is fullness of joy; at Your right hand are pleasures forevermore*" (Psalm 16:11, NKJV).
- "*Come, let us bow down in worship, let us kneel before the Lord our Maker*" (Psalm 95:6).

Fill your life with gratitude:

- *"Give thanks to the Lord, for he is good; his love endures forever"* (1 Chronicles 16:34).
- *"And whatever you do, whether in word or deed, do it all in the name of the Lord Jesus, giving thanks to God the Father through him"* (Colossians 3:17).
- *"Do not be anxious about anything, but in every situation, by prayer and petition, with thanksgiving, present your requests to God"* (Philippians 4:6).
- *"The Lord is my strength and my shield; my heart trusts in him, and he helps me. My heart leaps for joy, and with my song I praise him"* (Psalm 28:7).

Read and meditate on the Bible:

- *"Your word is a lamp to my feet and a light to my path"* (Psalm 119:105, NKJV).
- *"All Scripture is given by inspiration of God, and is profitable for doctrine, for reproof, for correction, for instruction in righteousness"* (2 Timothy 3:16, NKJV).
- *"Every word of God proves true; he is a shield to those who take refuge in him"* (Proverbs 30:5, ESV).
- *"The unfolding of your words gives light; it imparts understanding to the simple"* (Psalm 119:130).
- *"Do not merely listen to the word, and so deceive yourselves. Do what it says. Anyone who listens to the word but does not do what it says is like someone who looks at his face in a mirror and, after looking at himself, goes away and immediately forgets what he looks like. But whoever looks intently into the perfect law that gives freedom, and continues in it—not forgetting what*

they have heard, but doing it—they will be blessed in what they do" (James 1:22-25).

- Billy Graham said, "The very practice of reading [the Bible] will have a purifying effect upon your mind and heart. Let nothing take the place of this daily exercise."

Despite the distractions of this world and the busyness of life, we MUST return to the practices and personal disciplines of our fathers in the faith. We must build our spiritual immune systems so that our shields of faith are up and ready to quench every fiery dart of the enemy. (See Ephesians 6:16.) Infirmity cannot survive in the atmosphere of faith. Sickness withers and dies in the presence of Jesus. That's why we must continue with the best practices mentioned in the list above.

Through reading this devotional and doing the things I have outlined for your 30-day Healing Dare, you are building some serious faith muscle and nourishing your spiritual immune system! You are getting stronger. The Holy Spirit in you is being allowed to obliterate strongholds and illuminate your path. Your picture is changing.

You are doing a great job, and I'm so proud of you for sticking with it! Don't quit!

 **READ**

Luke 17:11-19

SELF-REFLECTION:

Write some things that you need to do more often to build your spirit. And remember, it's not about legalism; it's about a relationship with Love, Himself. Self-care may be all the buzz right now, but "spiritual care" is even more important!

 # TODAY'S TAKEAWAY:

I will build my spiritual immune system through fellowship with other believers, church attendance, joy, prayer, worship, gratitude, and Bible reading.

PRAYER

Holy Spirit, remind me to build my spirit each day, despite the busyness and distractions around me. Help me rearrange my priorities. I want to spend more time with You in the coming days.

REPAINT YOUR PICTURE

CONQUERING FEAR

DAY 17

The greatest enemy to building and keeping your eyes on a picture of faith is that old liar, fear. If faith is the language of God's Kingdom, fear is the language of the earth curse. Fear loves to speak when we are trying to stand in faith, because if it can get us to take our eyes off of Jesus, it can rob us of our blessing and victory.

Fear was a generational curse that I had to stand up to and break off of my own life.

I dealt with panic attacks, anxiety, and worry constantly when I was as young as seven years old. My dad was also dealing with panic attacks at the time. One night at the age of eight, I came to my mom, once again sobbing in fear. This happened every night. She said, "Enough is enough. It's time for you to speak God's Word and stand up to this." She then wrote out some Scriptures about victory through Jesus, His protection, and the freedom from fear that He paid for. She wrote at the top of the page, "Amy's Gos-pills" and she told me to take these daily or anytime I felt afraid.

She taped that sheet of Scriptures on the top of my canopy bed so I could see it every night when I lay down. That was when the voice of fear would try to speak. But instead of listening to it, I started saying those eight Scriptures out loud. I would say them over and over again until the scary feelings left and I could sleep.

Pretty soon, the voice of fear got quieter and quieter until it was gone. At a very young age, my parents taught me how to fight with the Word. And it worked!

That old spirit tried to come back when I started dealing with physical illness in my late teens into my early twenties. Everyone who has faced sickness knows what it's like. The devil tells you you're dying or that you'll always be this way even if you live. It's torment! But it's also just a really vivid illusion painted by the master deceiver. Be assured, whatever the spirit of fear says IS A LIE. I was reminded in my twenties that this enemy could not be reasoned with—it had to be kicked out.

Thank God that He has given us the name of Jesus as a weapon against those demonic spirits. When you speak that name with authority, fear MUST go. It has no individual choice, because the matter has been settled. Jesus won the final victory against fear when He rose from the dead. He took back the authority and gave it to us again, so that we can command fear to leave and it must obey. Fear MUST respond and leave when you enforce the victory Jesus already paid for on the cross! (We will talk more about how to enforce the victory soon.)

The apostle Paul said to, *"Fight the good fight of the faith"* (1 Timothy 6:12a). In other words, **the real fight isn't to "get healed"; it is simply to stay in faith.** If we can stay in faith (fully persuaded that God's promises are true, trusting Him like a child), we will have the fruit of what we ask for (John 14:13, John 15:5).

One day, my husband started having chest pains. He didn't think much about it, but it continued for several days, and on the third day, he finally told me about it. We decided to go get it checked out, but I told him before we walked into that medical facility, "No matter what they say, we know the Truth, and the Truth is you are healed!"

We came into agreement on that. The doctor ran an EKG, and everything seemed fine. But his blood work showed that there was distress in his body and that his blood wasn't clotting properly (in layman's terms). That's why the doctor said there was a strong chance he may have a blood clot in his chest. The medical staff got very serious then. The nurse told Jason, "Do not move. Do not get up from this bed. If that clot dislodges, you will die. You'll be dead."

Now doesn't that sound just like the devil?! I could see a shadow pass over Jason's countenance. I mean, that escalated quickly! For the record, I'm fine with medical professionals stating facts, but often they have been trained to tell you the worst possible scenario. You just have to be prepared for that. They are entitled to their professional opinion, and they have studied the effects of the earth curse on the body. But they are not God, and their word is not THE Word. There is still so much that science can't explain or understand.

The nurse hurried out of the room to prep the contrast dye CT scan they wanted to do to quickly confirm their suspicions. That's when I got angry at the enemy! I looked my husband squarely in the eye, grabbed his hand, and I said, "Jason, that is a lie from hell. You will live and not die, and you will declare the works of the Lord. You will have no fear of bad news, because your heart trusts confidently in the Lord" (Psalm 118:17, Psalm 112:7).

I then laid my hands on his chest and commanded any blood clots to dissolve, in the name of Jesus. We spoke the Word over his body until the doctor came to take him to the scan. The whole time he was gone, I had to fight the lie the devil had spoken through that nurse. Thoughts tried to hit me like, *What if he dies? You're gonna have to raise your kids alone as a single mother. He could have a massive stroke.*

But we had already prayed the prayer of faith over his body, and I wasn't having it. This was a total assault against our peace. I marched around that tiny exam room, praying in the Spirit and thanking God that it was finished. I ignored the waves of emotion that tried to come.

You may say, "Well, Amy, if you were in faith, why did those thoughts and feelings come?" Good question!

Know this: Just because you're standing in faith doesn't mean there aren't going to be thoughts and emotions that try to come to contradict the Truth.

The question is, will you fall for those emotions and thoughts?

Will you let them take control? Or will you contradict them with the Truth? What picture will you believe?

Our emotions are so fickle, and they are trained to respond to whatever stimuli is around. Sometimes you have to tell your emotions to shut up! And that's what I did that day in the hospital. My sister-in-law Alecia says that emotions are given to us by God to let us know where we are headed. Feeling fear might feel like a natural human response, but we have the option of getting off at the "exit of fear," or keeping on the "road of faith." Emotions are temporary and will change. Don't let them derail you. Keep your eyes on Jesus, and keep your head up! About halfway through my wait during Jason's CT scan, I felt total joy and peace wash over me. I knew that, *"All will be well with you and your children"* (Deuteronomy 4:40, NLT). My emotions came into alignment with God's Truth.

They finally brought Jason back into the exam room and said, "We did the scan twice, and nothing is there. Everything looks fine." Jason exclaimed, "Then we are going home!" He practically ran out of that hospital. Haha!

As we walked out, Jason said, "I just realized my chest has stopped hurting!" What had bothered him for three days was totally gone then, without medication or intervention. We had a little praise party on our drive home. Whether or not there was a blood clot or a health problem when we walked into that hospital made no difference, because he walked out totally healed. We refused to come into agreement with the scare tactic of the devil.

Stand Firm

Picture this: A stranded person in a boat out on a lake sends up a flare to attract someone his way. When another boater sees the flare and approaches, they hop on board the other boat to see what is the matter. But it was a trap. The "stranded" person jumps onto the working boat, steals it, and sails away into the sunset. That story is an illustration of this truth: **The devil sends up flares to try and attract us to a lie.** The devil wants us to divert our course off of God's path for our lives so that he can rob us of our destinies. He wants us to come into agreement with his mirages. **He wants us to change course and shipwreck on the rocks of fear.** That's when the Word must be our anchor.

When the devil throws wrong pictures our way—illusions and smokescreens—that try to convince us of a lie, like that nurse telling my husband, "You could drop dead at any minute," we turn our attention back to the Truth.

When he tries to paint the most outrageous pictures of defeat, we must speak the Word. We cannot come into agreement with the lie! We cannot get closer to inspect that lie, or spend time with that lie, or contemplate that lie. We should not Google the lie or research the possibilities of the lie.

When fear tries to act like a huge Doberman, remind yourself that it's just a little Chihuahua! Kick that yappy dog out! First Peter 5:8-9a say,

> *Be alert and of sober mind. Your enemy the devil prowls around* **_like_** *a roaring lion looking for someone to devour. Resist him,* **_standing firm in the faith_**.

Even though the devil acts LIKE a roaring lion, we know the Truth: Jesus is the Lion of the tribe of Judah! "...*Do not weep! See, the Lion of the tribe of Judah, the Root of David, has triumphed...*" (Revelation 5:5).

When fear paints the wrong picture, you must shut your eyes to those illusions, forget how your emotions are going crazy in the moment, and vehemently reject the lie with everything in you! Be a warrior, "*[looking away from all that will distract us and] focusing our eyes on Jesus*" (Hebrews 12:2a, AMP).

Faith rejects lies. Faith only sees the Truth. It gives no audience to the trickery of fear. It completely douses the flames of doubt. Paul also said, "*In addition to all this, take up the shield of faith, with which you can extinguish all the flaming arrows of the evil one*" (Ephesians 6:16). Faith shields us from the emotional torment and turmoil that fear tries to bring.

How do you raise your shield of faith? By believing and speaking ONLY what God has said about your situation.

When fear talks, you have to talk back, just like I did in that exam room. Don't allow fear to speak.

DON'T LET FEAR FINISH ITS SENTENCE.

Here are some of my favorite Scriptures concerning fear—the ones that my mom wrote down for me when I was that scared eight-year-old girl. God's Word changed my life then and has many times since. It holds the same power for you as well.

Scripture readings to defeat fear:

For God has not given us a spirit of fear, but of power and of love and of a sound mind.
—2 Timothy 1:7 (NKJV)

Don't be afraid, for I am with you. Don't be discouraged, for I am your God. I will strengthen you and help you. I will hold you up with my victorious right hand.
—Isaiah 41:10 (NLT)

Cast all your anxiety on him because he cares for you.
—1 Peter 5:7

So God has given both his promise and his oath. These two things are unchangeable because it is impossible for God to lie. Therefore, we who have fled to him for refuge can have great confidence as we hold to the hope that lies before us. This hope is a strong and trustworthy anchor for our souls. It leads us through the curtain into God's inner sanctuary. Jesus has already gone in there for us. He has become our eternal High Priest in the order of Melchizedek.

—Hebrews 6:18-20 (NLT)

Satan has asked for you, that he may sift you as wheat. But I have prayed for you, that your faith should not fail.

—Luke 22:31b-32a (NJKV)

Behold, I give you the authority to trample on serpents and scorpions, and over all the power of the enemy, and nothing shall by any means hurt you.

—Luke 10:19 (NKJV)

 # SELF-REFLECTION:

Choose one of the above Scriptures and write it out with your name in it.

 # TODAY'S TAKEAWAY:

I will not let the thief of fear rob me of my future. I have power and authority over the spirit of fear.

PRAYER

Lord Jesus, thank You for winning my victory over fear! I submit to You, resist the devil, and he must flee, according to James 4:7. I speak to fear and say, "GO NOW and never return, in the mighty name that's above every name, Jesus!"

STAND IN AUTHORITY

THE KINGDOM WAY

DAY 18

Welcome to the next step in your 30-day Healing Dare! We've already spent some time covering the first two steps:

1. Reclaim your identity. (Know who you are in Christ.)

2. Repaint your picture. (Faith is fully persuaded of God's promises.)

Now that you know who you are and understand what it means to have faith in God's promises, it's time to learn how to *receive* those promises and stand in your authority as a citizen of God's Kingdom.

In order to understand what I mean by this next key to receiving healing, I want to define some things so you have a visual picture.

When we became born again, we transferred our citizenship from the "nation of darkness" to the "nation of light," much like someone who immigrates from another country and becomes a citizen. My friend Sarah immigrated to the United States and became a legal citizen. Now she has all the rights and benefits that I do as a natural born citizen. As soon as an immigrant takes the nation's oath of citizenship, as my friend did, they are entitled to every right and protection that any other citizen of that nation receives.

We, too, have become citizens of the Kingdom of God, having immigrated out of the kingdom of darkness. We can now receive the promises of God, *"For he has rescued us from the dominion of darkness and brought us into the kingdom of the Son he loves"* (Colossians 1:13).

We have a whole new way of living. And we need to learn all about this new Kingdom's laws, language, benefits, etc. **Like any earthly nation or kingdom, the Kingdom of heaven has:**

- **Citizens:**
  - Definition: *A person owing loyalty to and entitled by birth or naturalization to the protection of a state or nation.*[6]

  - We have rights as citizens of God's Kingdom. The Bible says:

    > *What is mankind that you are mindful of them, a son of man that you care for him? You made them a little lower than the angels; you crowned them with glory and honor and put everything under their feet.*
    > —Hebrews 2:6b-8

- **An Official Language:**
  - Definition: *the language or one of the languages that is accepted by a country's government, is taught in schools, used in the courts of law.*[7]

  - The language of heaven is faith.

- **A Constitution:**
  - Definition: *the set of political principles by which a state or organization is governed, especially in relation to the rights of the people it governs.*[8]

---

[6] *American Heritage Dictionary of the English Language, Fifth Edition*
[7] *Cambridge Business English Dictionary*
[8] *Cambridge Business English Dictionary*

- The constitution of this Kingdom is the Bible. It includes a "Bill of Rights," in the form of God's promises, the history of our faith, and the stories of many who have gone before us. It includes the Words of God, Himself, and states His will for every citizen of His Kingdom.

- **Laws:**
  - Definition: *a rule, usually made by a government, that is used to order the way in which a society behaves. The system of rules of a particular country, group, or area of activity.*[9]

  - The most important law that sums up all others is:

    Love the Lord your God with all your heart and with all your soul and with all your strength and with all your mind; and, Love your neighbor as yourself.
    —Luke 10:27

- **The Government or Ruling Authority:**
  - Definition: *the leader of a country; the group of people who officially control a country.*[10]

  - Our ruling authorities are God, the Father; God, the Son; and God, the Holy Spirit.

---

[9] *Cambridge Business English Dictionary*
[10] *Cambridge Business English Dictionary*

- You can look at it like each of the Trinity represents a different aspect or "branch" of heaven's government. It's not an exact parallel, because God is "three in one," but we can see a different part of His character revealed through the work of each. Here's a way to think about it:

- God, the Father is the "Legislative Branch," the branch that has the primary power to make the country's laws. God formed the laws that govern the natural world and the spiritual world (Job 38). God handed down the Ten Commandments to Moses (Exodus 20:2-17). He cannot break His own decrees and laws (Hebrews 6:18).

- God, the Son is similar to the "Judicial Branch," the branch that interprets and enforces the laws. When Jesus came, He enforced God's will on the earth, and He is now in the courts of heaven making intercession for us. That means He is pleading our case. His blood cries mercy. He established a new way to interpret our lives, through the knowledge of His grace.

> *And to Jesus, the Mediator (Go-between, Agent) of a New Covenant, and to the sprinkled blood which speaks [of mercy], a better and nobler and more gracious message than the blood of Abel [which cried out for vengeance].*
>
> —Hebrews 12:24 (AMPC)

Jesus became the lens through which we could see the Kingdom of heaven. He said over and over again, "The Kingdom of heaven is like…."

- God, the Holy Spirit is like the "Executive Branch," which is the branch that has the power to enforce or carry out the laws of the nation. The Spirit gives us power to fulfill our assignments, and He is on the earth now, enforcing what was accomplished by Jesus.

- **Public Servants:**
  - Definition: *A person who holds a government position by election or appointment.*[11]

  - We are all given spiritual giftings and appointed to different parts of the body for public service to our King. There are nine spiritual giftings given to citizens to carry out the King's wishes on Earth (1 Corinthians 12:8-10).

  - We are all ambassadors for the heavenly Kingdom, showing others the goodwill of our King.

  - There are also five authoritative offices of God's government in the earth realm: pastors, teachers, evangelists, prophets, and apostles. The local church is part of God's government, as He has ordained "shepherds" over His "flock."

---

[11] *Cambridge Business English Dictionary*

- **<u>Civil Rights</u>:**
  - Definition: *The rights belonging to an individual by virtue of citizenship.*[12]

  - There are many benefits to being a citizen, the best of which is freedom from spiritual death. We have redemption from sin and protection from our enemies. Other benefits include what David said in Psalm 103:2-6 (NKJV):

    > *Bless the Lord, O my soul, and forget not all His benefits: who forgives all your iniquities, who heals all your diseases, who redeems your life from destruction, who crowns you with lovingkindness and tender mercies, who satisfies your mouth with good things, so that your youth is renewed like the eagle's. The Lord executes righteousness and justice for all who are oppressed.*

  - The apostle Peter talked about our rights as precious promises:

    > *And because of his glory and excellence, he has given us great and precious promises. These are the promises that enable you to share his divine nature and escape the world's corruption caused by human desires.*
    >
    > —2 Peter 1:4 (NLT)

---

[12] *Cambridge Business English Dictionary*

- ***An Army***:
  - Definition: *A large body of people organized and trained for warfare.*[13]

  - Angels are the army of God and are here to protect citizens and do God's will on Earth.

  - *"The angel of the Lord encamps around those who fear Him, and rescues them"* (Psalm 34:7, NASB).

  - *"For He will give His angels orders concerning you, to protect you in all your ways"* (Psalm 91:11).

What a wonderful thing to be a citizen of this great Kingdom of heaven with Jehovah God as our Ruler and Sovereign King! Plus, with it comes all of His precious promises to us. As Pastor Miles Monroe said, "Citizenship is not a right; it's a privilege, but once you are a citizen, you have rights." I'm so thankful for that!

Unlike earthly kingdoms, this Kingdom cannot be corrupted or defeated. Hebrews 12:28 say:

> *Therefore, since we are receiving a kingdom <u>that cannot be shaken</u>, let us be thankful, and so worship God acceptably with reverence and awe.*

As we learn the Kingdom way of living, and use the tools God has given us, we find our courage. Why? Because when we know how the government of God works and what rights have been given to all of His subjects, we can take a stand against violators, intruders, and

---

[12] *Cambridge Business English Dictionary*

trespassers. We can demand justice. The enemy, satan, has no legal right to steal, kill, or destroy; and if he tries, we can go after him in the name of Jesus. Spiritual authority requires knowledge of what rightfully belongs to us.

Since I'm an American citizen with rights, if someone broke into my house and stole thousands of dollars' worth of things, I could call the police. I could use our legal system to prosecute that person and demand justice. In the same way, as citizens of heaven, we can demand that the devil stop stealing what rightfully belongs to us—including our health. We can say, "Back off, devil! This body is God's property!"

Is there a thief in your house? Have you failed to stand up to that thief? Perhaps you haven't known your authority as God's representative on Earth, authorized to use the Word of God against the devil. But now you know the foundation of how the Kingdom of God is set up. Now that you have this understanding of this new Kingdom we are a part of, let's talk about how to enforce our victory and take authority over the spirit of infirmity in the next devotion. Let's stop this thief in his tracks!

 **READ**

Acts 26:18

 **DETOX:**
What wrong beliefs about God's principles and His Kingdom have you had in the past? Has there been a thief in your house?

SELF-REFLECTION:

What are some ways in which you exercise your rights as a citizen of your country? How does this apply or not apply to God's Kingdom?

TODAY'S TAKEAWAY:

I am a child of God and a co-heir with Christ. That position of citizenship comes with authority, rights, and benefits, including healing.

PRAYER

Father God, help me understand the Kingdom way of living life, so that I can represent You and Your will here. Help me to stand up in courage, for it's only through You that any of this is possible, and without You I cannot do anything. You are my Sovereign King and Lord of my life.

STAND IN AUTHORITY

AUTHORITY GIVEN

DAY 19

When my husband was young, he had a friend named Josh, whom he often invited over to play basketball. However, Jason's mom started to get a bad feeling about the kid, so she told him to stop hanging around Josh.

A few weeks later, Jason came home to find the front door standing wide open and the house ransacked and burglarized. It was a mess! He called his parents, who immediately called the police.

Now according to the law, it is illegal to steal or destroy someone else's property, so the law enforcement officers immediately went to work to reclaim what was stolen. Jason felt that Josh might be the culprit, since he knew how to get into their house, so the police started there. They paid a visit to Josh's house.

Sure enough, the police found that Josh was still in possession of the stolen items that he had not sold yet, and he made a full confession. Most of the stolen items were recovered. Why? Because the police enforced the law meant to protect citizens from theft.

In the same way, it's our job to help enforce the laws of the New Covenant that Jesus gave us. Remember, the New Covenant is the list of "I will if you will" items that we studied earlier. That New Covenant promises protection against the evil one, which prohibits him from touching us or our stuff. The devil may want to steal, kill, and destroy God's property (John 10:10), but HE HAS NO AUTHORITY. That doesn't mean he isn't going to try. It means that when he tries, you call foul and demand justice. You demand that he leave and return all that was stolen.

The devil is a thief, but he must repay seven times over what he has stolen. Now, is a thief going to enforce the law against him? Is he going to turn himself in and say, "Go ahead; prosecute me to the full extent of the law?" Nope! He's going to hide, work in the shadows, and try to conceal who is really doing the dirty work and who is guilty. Perhaps the devil has been doing the same to you—stealing but making it look as if it's someone else's fault. Perhaps you've even blamed yourself, saying, "Maybe I did something wrong. Maybe I should have done such and such better. Maybe God is punishing me." But wouldn't the thief, the devil, love to remain hidden and blame others, have you blame yourself, or have you blame God? It's not in the devil's nature to tell the Truth. That's why you have to be the Truth Teller and Kingdom enforcer in every situation. You have to call him out, expose him in the daylight, and demand justice.

I love this promise: "'*But I will restore you to health and heal your wounds,' declares the Lord*" (Jeremiah 30:17a). God shall restore all that the enemy has tried to do in your life. And you can demand justice against the thief! He must repay seven times what he stole in terms of health, time, relationships, finances, etc. The Bible says about a thief, "*But when he is found, he must repay seven times [what he stole]; he must give all the property of his house [if necessary to meet his fine]*" (Proverbs 6:31 AMP). It's up to you and me to find the thief, call him out, and demand justice. It's God's job to restore when we trust Him.

Using Our Authority

We've been given authority on the earth, based on some of the Scriptures we have already read that talk about humankind's created place of honor and authority. But just because we *have* something doesn't mean we know how to *use* it. I sure didn't. I knew I was sick and

God promised health, but I wasn't sure how to stop the spirits of infirmity, self-hatred, shame, and fear from stealing from me. It started with discovering those spirits, finding them out. The Holy Spirit showed me who was behind all of the theft going on in my life at the time. Then I had to do something about it. That's when God started showing me how to take my authority and use it. To "take authority" means to confidently enforce the victory already given to us on the cross. Just like police officers enforce the law of the land against a house intruder, we must enforce the victory already given to us against the devil's plans.

Your body, my friend, is God's property. First Corinthians 6:19 (NKJV) says, *"Do you not know that your body is a temple of the Holy Spirit, who is in you, whom you have received from God? You are not your own."* If your body is God's temple, the devil has no right to come in, ransack it, steal things from it, and tear it down.

In other words, the spirit of infirmity is illegally trespassing on God's property! Now, when that happens, we have two choices. We can give in. Run in fear. Surrender. *Or* we can stand up and kick that demon out, enforce the law, and bring that thief to justice.

How do we do that? There's a story from the life of Jesus in Matthew 8:5-13 (NLT) that perfectly illustrates this picture of authority:

> *When Jesus returned to Capernaum, a Roman officer came and pleaded with him, "Lord, my young servant lies in bed, paralyzed and in terrible pain." Jesus said, "I will come and heal him." But the officer said, "Lord, I am not worthy to have you come into my home. <u>Just say the word</u> from where you are, and my servant will be healed. I know this because <u>I am under the</u>*

authority of my superior officers, and I have authority over my soldiers. I only need to say, 'Go,' and they go, or 'Come,' and they come. And if I say to my slaves, 'Do this,' they do it."

When Jesus heard this, he was amazed. Turning to those who were following him, he said, "I tell you the truth, I haven't seen faith like this in all Israel! And I tell you this, that many Gentiles will come from all over the world—from east and west—and sit down with Abraham, Isaac, and Jacob at the feast in the Kingdom of Heaven. But many Israelites—those for whom the Kingdom was prepared—will be thrown into outer darkness, where there will be weeping and gnashing of teeth." Then Jesus said to the Roman officer, "Go back home. Because you believed, it has happened." And the young servant was healed that same hour.

So here's a leader in the Roman army, a Gentile without a covenant, but he understands the authority of Jesus. He understands military command and rank. And he knows that Jesus can pull rank over demon spirits, including the spirit of infirmity. The soldier understood authority. When a commanding officer gives an order, even if from another location, the lower troops snap to attention and follow orders.

I'm sure the disciples and other Jews with Jesus were a bit put off by this guy, who to them represented Roman domination over Israel. But Jesus doesn't participate in religious divisions, racial divisions, petty disagreements, or human arguments. He cares about people, and He responds to faith.

Even though Jesus offered to go to the Centurion's house, this soldier knew and understood that Jesus only needed to send His Word to heal his servant. Perhaps he had heard the Psalm of David that says, *"He sent out his word and healed them; he rescued them from the grave"* (Psalm 107:20). Jesus was amazed that this guy got spiritual authority and had such faith. This Roman put his faith in the One who holds all power. And his servant was healed the moment Jesus commanded it to be so. Why? Because **Jesus pulls the highest rank in the spirit realm.** All demonic hosts pale in comparison to His matchless authority. He is the final word. If He gives a command, it's done.

Now we know we can do the same. You might think, "Amy, are you saying we can do the same thing Jesus did?! Isn't that a bit presumptuous?" Not if we do it according to His will, walking in the power He gave us. The following are Jesus's words, not mine:

> *Very truly I tell you, whoever believes in me will do the works I have been doing, and they will do even greater things than these, because I am going to the Father. And I will do whatever you ask in my name, so that the Father may be glorified in the Son. You may ask me for anything in my name, and I will do it.*
>
> —John 14:12-14

In other words, we have been given His name, which is the highest ranking name in the spiritual realm. When we speak His name in faith, the spiritual realm snaps to attention and does what is commanded. In Matthew 16:19, Jesus said:

> *I will give you the keys of the kingdom of heaven; and whatever you bind on earth shall have been bound in heaven, and whatever you loose on earth shall have been loosed in heaven.*

God backs up and enforces whatever we back up and enforce. Jesus has essentially deputized us to be His representatives on the earth. He is not here in the flesh, as He was when the disciples were alive, but He is here with us through the Holy Spirit. We have legal access to His power, the same power Jesus used to heal the sick.

No, this is not some kind of New Age healing power. This is the authorization from heaven for us to enforce God's will on the earth. We can pull rank in the spirit realm and command demonic hosts to leave, by the authority that comes with the name of Jesus. Therefore, we can say, "Spirit of infirmity, leave my body and stop causing destruction here. This is God's property, so you are trespassing! This is a violation of my legal rights as a citizen of heaven, so you have no choice but to go!"

I like the way Rick Pina describes the keys in the story of the Centurion:

> The Centurion understood authority. He knew that if he commanded anyone that he had authority over to do something, they had to do it. The Centurion perceived that Jesus had authority over sickness. The Centurion knew that the person in authority does not have to be present to exercise rule. Just like he could "send a word" to another soldier to do something, He knew that Jesus could simply "speak the word only" for healing. His faith extended beyond his sight. If you can see something, then it does not require faith. The Centurion spoke His desired outcome. The language of faith does not limit itself to what it sees or to the present situation. The language of faith speaks those things that are not as though they were (Romans 4:17). In other words, the lan-

<u>guage of faith understands the situation but speaks the solution and not the problem</u>. The language of faith always looks forward in faith and never backwards in doubt.

You have been deputized and authorized to say, "Go!" and the devil must go. You can say to the good thing you need, "Come!" and it must come. The authority you have been given comes straight from the top. The victory you already have far outmatches the thief's cunning plans. Just call him out and demand justice!

READ

Job 22:27-28

DETOX:

Grab a sheet of paper and make a list of things you know were stolen by the thief, satan. This could include physical things such as a house, and it could include intangibles such as peace. Take that list before the Lord and ask Him for a full restoration of all that was stolen. Then tell the thief, "The Lord rebukes you, devil. You must repay seven times what you have stolen."

SELF-REFLECTION:

Think about a time you stood up for yourself and took authority against an injustice or wrong treatment. What gave you the courage to speak up or act?

TODAY'S TAKEAWAY:

I will use my God-given authority to speak to the circumstances of my life.

PRAYER

Lord, You said that I could decree a thing and see it done. You have put Your love in my heart and Your authority in my life, so I receive that power from the Holy Spirit to cause change, to speak faith, and to watch You move.

STAND IN AUTHORITY

CONFIDENCE IN GOD'S CHARACTER

I know a lot of Christians who aren't sure if it's God's will to heal. Heck, they don't even know the heart and character of God. They are afraid God might be angry at them or out to get them. They live in fear of punishment and are constantly waiting for something bad to happen. They don't know the goodness of God. I dealt with this a lot in *Healed Overnight*, but I want to share it here, because this is absolutely CRUCIAL.

If we don't know God's character, we will not be able to stand on His promises. And if we don't know if we can count on His promises, we are without hope. We have no way to counter satan's attacks. We end up living lives that are just as powerless and purposeless as unbelievers.

Fatalistic Christians

If we think there's a chance God causes or allows sickness to teach us a lesson, we must simply accept whatever fate comes our way. I've heard people say, "Well it must have been their time to go," or "God needed another rose for His garden." I call this "Christian fatalism." This attitude reminds me of the Doris Day song that says: "Que sera sera, whatever will be, will be. The future's not ours to see. Que sera, sera."

Christians literally walk through life saying, "Whatever will be, will be."

In not knowing what to accept as God's will, these Christians accept *everything* that comes their way as if it's God's will. By not knowing God's blessings, they accept the devil's curses. Isn't that exactly what satan would love? He wants to cut us off from our Source. In a manipulative twisting of the Truth, the deceiver questions God's character and accuses God of the very thing he, himself has done. He wants to throw shade. He wants people to think it's God, not him, who is killing, stealing, and destroying.

Now, I don't blame most fatalistic Christians for their confusion and misconceptions, because many churches, songs, and websites all contain these blasphemous accusations against God's character, disguised in nice, neat little words like "sovereignty" and "cessationism" and "judgment." We will talk about those in a minute. Fatalistic Christians just don't know the Truth due to false teaching and not getting into the Word themselves.

Some people base this fatalistic viewpoint on the doctrine about the sovereignty of God that says God will arbitrarily do whatever He feels like doing in any given situation. Supposedly, this also means we can't really ever be sure of His will. The word *sovereignty* means:

- Supremacy of authority or rule as exercised by a sovereign or sovereign state.
- Royal rank, authority, or power.
- Complete independence and self-government.[14]

Is God sovereign? Yes. But in His sovereignty, He has established laws and made choices that He will not violate. In the beginning of Jesus's ministry, in His first sermon that we read from Isaiah 61, it starts with, "*The Spirit of the Sovereign Lord is upon me.*" Jesus was declaring to all that the Sovereign God sent Him. In God's independent supremacy of authority, He made the choice to send Jesus and establish the New Covenant with us. He established laws and principles that

---

[14] *The American Heritage® Dictionary of the English Language, Fifth Edition*

He will not go back on. He will not violate His own Word. God will not double back on His promises. He doesn't make one rule or promise one day and then change it the next.

Not Your Time to Go

So how can we *know* it's God's will for us to keep on living? While we will all graduate to eternity at some point, if we aren't satisfied with a long life, then IT'S NOT TIME TO GO. When a diagnosis from a doctor comes, or symptoms present themselves, we must not get caught in a fatalistic mentality! Sure, it can cause emotions of fear, hopelessness, and thoughts of death. But if you haven't finished your race, STAY! Psalm 91:16 says, *"With long life I will satisfy him and show him my salvation."* We all have a race to run and an assignment to complete.

Don't let the devil talk you off of your purpose for living. You are needed, created for a mission on Earth. God destined you to be born for such a time as this.

When you face a difficult situation in your health or otherwise, it's crucial to hang on to your WHY so you don't get fatalistic. And when it is truly time for you to go home to Jesus, with a full heart and satisfied life, you can be like my great-grandma. She was ready. She wasn't sick, even though she was in her 80s. She just went to sleep one night, and my great-grandpa found her the next morning with a sweet, peaceful look on her face—with Jesus.

Lazy Christians

Some of the saddest television shows are the ones that show people who are morbidly obese, can't get around, and yet they just won't do what their doctors are telling them. They won't stop eating. They won't get up and move. So they die way too young. They remind me of the second category of Christians who don't receive anything from God. Along with the fatalistic Christians, who just don't *know* the will of God, we have the lazy Christians, who just won't *do* the will of God. Lazy Christians are not doers of the Word. They want someone else to prepare their meals for them and spoon feed them. They want a quick fix without commitment or perseverance attached. They don't like to think they have a role to play in things. They are unwilling to take personal responsibility for their own mistakes, lack of understanding, or weak faith. They just "leave it up to God" while continuing to feed on junk, sin, negativity, and self-pity.

Lazy Christians find it easier to blame their church or pastor or family for not doing more for them. They often get offended by the Truth and leave their churches. They complain that the devil has been on their case, yet they do nothing to stop him. They talk more about their problems than their God. They are too weak from inaction to put up any fight. Often, this type of person doesn't truly want to get well because, deep down inside, they like the attention and sympathy they receive due to their illness. Ouch. But it's true for some.

We can believe in God all day, but faith without works is dead (James 2:26). If we don't do the will of God, take action, and enforce the victory paid for on the cross, we still won't see the will of God in our lives. We've got to do something. We need to move our hearts closer to Jesus. We need to speak the Truth out loud. Worship. Demand justice. Feed on the Scriptures. Get ourselves out of bed and into church. Love on the lost. Feed the poor. Focus on others. Give generously. Tithe. Walk in love in our marriages. These are all principles that were established to bring about good in our lives. Yet, they require action.

Are you in one of those categories—a fatalistic Christian or lazy Christian? Then let's get you out! It's not hard: simply find God's will in His Word and then start doing it!

Is God a Child Abuser?

I've heard songs on the radio that imply God has done some awful thing, such as kill a baby. One such song says:

> Two months is too little. They let him go. They had no sudden healing. To think that Providence would take a child from his mother while she prays is appalling. Who told us we'd be rescued?

I'm sorry, but this is disgusting. We call parents that harm their children "child abusers," and God is not a child abuser. Providence did not take the child! It's blatant character slander. The Prince of Wales won a huge lawsuit against a newspaper for character defamation. Why? It's illegal to slander someone's character by telling lies.

So if God is not into abusing His kids, why is there so much of this demonic propaganda in the church that blames God for what the devil is doing? Because satan is crafty, and he lies about God's character to everyone. While God *mourns* for people who suffer, and wishes they would know His heart for them, satan works overtime to make people believe it must be God who causes or allows their pain. In actuality, God has higher standards for blessing His kids than *we* human parents do.

Jesus said:

> *"Which of you fathers, if your son asks for a fish, will give him a snake instead? Or if he asks for an egg, will give him a scorpion?* <u>*If you then, though you are evil, know how to give good gifts to your children, how much more will your Father in heaven give the Holy Spirit to those who ask him!*</u>*"*
>
> —Luke 11:11-13

We, as humans, want good things for our kids. We love buying them that one toy they are so excited about for Christmas. We think of ways to bless them. We love to see them smile. So does God!

One day I was holding my daughter and tickling her. She was laughing that adorable belly laugh that kids have. I then heard God whisper to my heart, *"That's My favorite, too, when My children are in My arms, laughing, filled with joy."*

He doesn't wish sorrow or pain on us. Nor does He use darkness to bring light. He doesn't cause bad to then bring good. He's not schizophrenic. He does, however, turn around bad situations that we have brought on ourselves or that the devil has tried to use against us, or that people have perpetuated. He can even redeem those situations!

Joseph, who once was abused and sold into slavery by his own brothers, had become second only to Pharoah, ruler of Egypt. It was a long journey, but because Joseph trusted God, he was promoted to high honor out of a dark situation. He said this to his brothers, the very men who devastated him: *"You tried to harm me, but God made it turn out for the best, so that he could save all these people, as he is now doing"* (Genesis 50:20, CEV).

You see, the devil will use people to try and hurt us. People are going to do stuff that is just plain evil. But even in those situations, God will vindicate us, elevate us, promote us, and bless us, just as He did for Joseph, if we will keep our lives focused on Him.

People try to use this Scripture to say that God brings good <u>and</u> bad: *"And we know that in all things God works for the good of those who love him, who have been called according to his purpose"* (Romans 8:28). But it doesn't say ALL things come from God. It says IN all things.

IN a bad situation, God is still able to bring good out of it.

IN the midst of the mess, He can turn it around.

For instance, out of my sickness, I have been able to share my story and see many healed. Does that mean that God put the sickness on me in the first place, to bring good in the end? No, <u>God doesn't use an "ends-justifies-the-means" approach to parenting</u>. Even we humans know that's terrible ethics.

Some people have been taught that sickness glorifies God. They often take that thought from the story below. Jesus and His disciples saw a blind man alongside the road, and during that time, many people thought that people were born sick because of some hidden sin, so the disciples ask Jesus about that:

And His disciples asked Him, saying, "Rabbi, who sinned, this man or his parents, that he was born blind?" Jesus answered, "Neither this man nor his parents sinned, but that the works of God should be revealed in him. I must work the works of Him who sent Me while it is day; the night is coming when no one can work. As long as I am in the world, I am the light of the world"

—John 9:2-5 (NKJV)

Jesus answers them and says that He must work the works of Him who sent Him, and then He healed the blind man. So the work of God was for him to be healed! Jesus came as the light to our fallen, sin-soaked, disease-ridden world. He came to reveal the work of God to this man and heal Him. Jesus was saying, "Look, guys, forget about pointing fingers of blame. The important thing is that the Word of God be revealed in Him. Let me show you what I mean." Bam! Healed!

Another interesting thing to note is that in Hebrew, there is no punctuation. What happens when you remove the period in this Scripture and replace it with a comma?

But that the works of God should be revealed in him, I must work the works of Him who sent Me while it is still day....

Sounds a little bit different, doesn't it? Just saying...

The point is, in order to see the Truth, we must see through the correct lens. We must see through the lens that God is always good. We must be confident and fully persuaded that He is kind. Here are some Scriptures showing some attributes of God's character:

- **God is light:** *"This is the message we have heard from him and declare to you: <u>God is light; in him there is no darkness at all</u>"* (1 John 1:5). Is sickness a form of darkness? Absolutely! It is cells literally going dark. So invite the light of God into your cells and every fiber of your being.

- **God is good:** *"The Lord is <u>good to all</u>; he has compassion on all he has made"* (Psalm 145:9). Is sickness good? Not for the person that is sick! So today, welcome the goodness of God to work in your body, hold you, help you, and heal you.

- **God is love:** *"The one who does not love has not become acquainted with God [does not and never did know Him], <u>for God is love. [He is the originator of love, and it is an enduring attribute of His nature]</u>"* (1 John 4:8, AMP). Is sickness a form of love? Often, sickness is either a foreign invader (such as a virus) or it is when the cells start attacking each other (like in autoimmune disorders). That doesn't sound like love to me. Invite God's love to fill your body and cause peace where there has been inflammation, acceptance where there has been rejection, and victory where there has been war.

- **God is faithful:** *"The steadfast love of the Lord never ceases; his mercies never come to an end; they are new every morning; <u>great is your faithfulness</u>"* (Lamentations 3:22-23). Is sickness a sign of God's faithfulness? No. That doesn't make sense, even to those who aren't Christians. Often, they see a failure of God's faithfulness. But it's never God's faithfulness that is lacking. His will for us to be healed has never changed. He is constant. He doesn't change His mind. Numbers 23:19 says,

"God is not a man, that He should lie, nor a son of man, that He should repent; has He said, and will He not do it? Or has He spoken, and will He not make it good?" Right now, let go of all doubts and all stress. Picture yourself relaxing in the arms of Jesus. He is holding you. He won't let you go.

- **God is compassionate:** *"For the Lord your God is a <u>compassionate</u> God; He will not fail you <u>nor destroy you</u> nor forget the covenant with your fathers which He swore to them"* (Deuteronomy 4:31, NASB). If we truly knew the wonderful heart of our Father, we would never fail to trust Him. Think of the kindest, most compassionate person you have ever known. Now, multiply that times a trillion. That's how amazingly GOOD our Father is. Take a minute to thank Father God for His loving compassion toward you. Let His acceptance flood your body. Let His merciful kindness permeate your heart.

In summary, God has a plan for our lives, but it's up to us to believe it and take action. We can believe that God is good and that He is to be trusted.

Job 22:27-28

What misconceptions about God's character are you getting rid of today? Has your relationship with your own father helped or hurt your view of God?

SELF-REFLECTION:

We are 20 days in! Let's set some faith goals for the final 10 days. Let's finish strong in building our faith and doing our part to be good receivers. This might look like stressing less, building more margins into your daily routine to allow for meditation on the Word of God, or starting to receive a small victory in your health from God along the way to the big victory.

 # TODAY'S TAKEAWAY:

God is GOOD, only good and ALWAYS good! I will not walk in fatalism or complacency, but instead I will trust God's character and be a doer of the Word.

PRAYER

Father, as Your child, I want to have a deeper relationship with You, and I want to know You more. Help me to walk with You day by day and trust that Your plans for me are good. I will look at You through the lens of Your overflowing kindness instead of seeing You as angry, distant, or unpredictable. In Jesus's mighty name, I come before You today, and I receive Your goodness toward me. Amen.

STAND IN AUTHORITY

CONFIDENCE IN GOD'S WILL

I have no problem admitting I was not in faith for healing for all those years of sickness. I was double-minded, going back and forth from faith to fear. The problem was on my end. *I was letting life happen to me instead of speaking life to what was happening.*

God didn't condemn me, but instead, He worked with me. My lack of faith was NOT an indication that God was lacking power. The problem was on my end of the deal, not His. He led me to the Truth when I cried out and asked for help and understanding, just like it says in James 1:

> *If any of you lacks wisdom [to guide him through a decision or circumstance], he is to ask of [our benevolent] God, who gives to everyone generously and without rebuke or blame, and it will be given to him. But he must ask [for wisdom] in faith, without doubting [God's willingness to help], for the one who doubts is like a billowing surge of the sea that is blown about and tossed by the wind. For such a person ought not to think or expect that he will receive anything [at all] from the Lord, being a double-minded man, unstable and restless in all his ways [in everything he thinks, feels, or decides].*
>
> —James 1:5-8 (AMP)

The Bible calls a person who doubts "double-minded" and says that person can't receive anything.

Picture this: I go into an ice cream shop with my child and offer to buy them some. I ask my child which flavor they want, but their response is, "I don't know if I want chocolate or vanilla. Maybe strawberry. Actually, I'm not sure I want ice cream. What if it isn't good? What if you poisoned it or something? What if you don't give it to me? How do I know you actually want to buy me some, Mom?"

My child is going to walk out of that shop empty-handed.

That's how many people talk to God about healing—He has offered it to them, but they flip-flop around in unbelief.

So let me ask you some questions:

- Why would God send Jesus to Earth to defeat death, and then author death in our lives?
- Why would God send Jesus to pay the price for pain and sickness, and then give us or allow what He came to save us from?
- Was Jesus's sacrifice on the cross enough for everything you and I would face? Did it apply to every illness and infirmity? Was His blood not costly enough to cover it all?
- If Jesus was the perfect representation of God's will, as it says in John 5:19, can we know the will of God through Jesus's example?
- Did Jesus ever turn someone away and tell them, "No!" when they asked for healing?
- Did Jesus ever put sickness on someone?
- Did Jesus ever represent Father God as a cruel child abuser?

Let's answer some of those questions with the Bible, not with the traditions of men. Instead of just blindly accepting doctrines taught by men, let's take personal responsibility to get into the Word, just like you are doing right now.

Find the Truth for yourself. Don't take my word for it either!

Jesus represented Father God's character and will perfectly. Jesus came to show us the way. Therefore, we CAN know God's will through Jesus.

> *So Jesus explained himself at length. "I'm telling you this straight. <u>The Son can't independently do a thing, only what he sees the Father doing</u>. What the Father does, the Son does."*
>
> —John 5:19a (MSG)

> *The Son is the radiance of God's glory and <u>the exact representation of his being</u>, sustaining all things by his powerful word. After he had provided purification for sins, he sat down at the right hand of the Majesty in heaven.*
>
> —Hebrews 1:3

Okay, so if Jesus was the walking, talking, living, breathing example of God's will on Earth, then we can know God's will through Jesus's example. And remember that God sovereignly chose to send Jesus to show us His love. So what did Jesus do about sickness and disease? He healed them. Always.

> *Jesus came down the mountain with the cheers of the crowd still ringing in his ears. Then a leper appeared and went to his knees before Jesus, praying, "Master, if you want to, you can heal my body." Jesus reached out and touched him, saying, "**I want to**. Be clean." Then and there, all signs of the leprosy were gone.*
>
> —Matthew 8:1-3 (MSG)

Jesus wanted to heal people. When the leper came to Him asking for healing, Jesus didn't say, "Let me think about it," or "Yeah, that's not my will." He said, "I want to!" Another translation says, "I will." Jesus indicated, "It's my will to heal." And if it was Jesus's will for that guy, it is His will for you today. It's Father God's will for you too.

Remember, God doesn't play favorites. What He did for me and for others in the Bible, He is bound by His Word to do for all who believe in Him. There are so many stories of Jesus healing people, but here's one Scripture that sums it all up:

> *How God anointed Jesus of Nazareth with the Holy Spirit and power, and how he went around <u>doing good and healing all</u> who were under the power of the devil, because God was with him.*
>
> —Acts 10:38

He did good and healed ALL.

Say this: "Jesus wants to do good to me and heal me. Father God wants to do good to me and heal me."

The Law of Death vs. The Law of Life

Every person born on Earth is subject to the Law of Sin and Death. It's the earth curse way of living we've been talking about. Let's refer back to Romans 8:2 (TPT):

> *For the "law" of the Spirit of life flowing through the anointing of Jesus has liberated us from the "law" of sin and death.*

God can't operate using the Law of Sin and Death. He can only operate in the Law of Life. Otherwise, He would be breaking His Word. He would be fighting against Himself! He is the Author of life. He doesn't use plays from satan's playbook.

The religious people of Jesus's day tried to accuse Him of doing just that, but Jesus said, *"No city or house divided against itself will stand. If Satan casts out Satan, he is divided against himself. How then will his kingdom stand?"* (Matthew 12:25b-26, ESV).

In other words, God can't use evil to accomplish His will, or He would be fighting against Himself, just like Jesus wasn't using evil powers to cast out demons.

Jesus came to save us from our infirmities, just like He came to save us from our sin. Again, He doesn't use something as a tool against us that He came to rescue us from.

Either His sacrifice was enough for *everything* or it was all for *nothing*. He either paid for the *entirety* of the earth curse that came upon mankind at the Fall, or He eliminated *none* of it.

Galatians 3:13-14 talk about Jesus taking the curse upon Himself to set us free from it:

> *Christ redeemed us from the curse of the law by becoming a curse for us, for it is written: "Cursed is everyone who is hung on a pole." He redeemed us in order that the blessing given to Abraham might come to the Gentiles through Christ Jesus, so that by faith we might receive the promise of the Spirit.*

So all of the curse was paid off. That includes sickness and poverty!

Read Genesis 3:16-19 for the curse that came on the earth, and know that now you can walk above that curse by walking in the Spirit, according to Romans 8!

Jesus Never Said No

Jesus never turned someone away or told them, "No," when they asked for healing in faith. He never told someone, "God is allowing this to teach you a lesson." He never insinuated, "This sickness is a good thing; we are going to leave it a little while longer."

As long as people believed in Him, they were healed. Abraham believed that God was able to give him a son, even when it looked impossible. His faith qualified him to receive. *"Abraham believed God, and it was credited to him as righteousness"* (Romans 4:3b). Abraham believed God and received the promises. We, too, can believe and receive the promises found in the New Covenant.

The Bible does say that Jesus was held back from doing many healings in just one place: His own hometown. But that wasn't because He didn't want to, or that God didn't love those people just as much as the others. There was another reason. The Bible says:

> *And they took offense at him. But Jesus said to them, "A prophet is not without honor except in his own town and in his own home." And he did not do many miracles there because of their lack of faith.*
>
> —Matthew 13:57-58

So the problem was on their end, not on His end. His will was the same for them as it was for the many hundreds of others whom He healed. But He could not violate their belief. He could not violate their free will. And those people could not receive from whom they didn't honor. They had no honor for Jesus because they grew up with Him. And thus, they stayed in their suffering. In contrast, there were many in other towns who chased after Jesus, believed in His power, and they received healing:

> *They ran throughout that whole region and carried the sick on mats to wherever they heard he was. And wherever he went—into villages, towns or countryside—they placed the sick in the marketplaces. They begged him to let them touch even the edge of his cloak, and **<u>all who touched it were healed</u>**.*
>
> —Mark 6:55-56

Still for Today?

People who believe in something called "cessationism" say that the things Jesus did on Earth and the things He told the disciples to do have mysteriously ceased happening.

Maybe you have been taught, "Healing passed away with the disciples." But why would only certain things pass away with the disciples? With this logic, we might as well say that everything else Jesus taught about and demonstrated also passed away with the disciples. There is no evidence in the New Testament that anything Jesus said would not endure, even until the end of the age.

<u>Either everything Jesus did and said will endure forever, or none of it will.</u>

In fact, in Matthew 24:35, Jesus said, *"Heaven and earth will pass away, but my words will never pass away."* This stands in direct opposition to the doctrine of cessationism. There are so many miracle healing stories in today's world, it just about does away with the thought that God stopped doing what He did through the disciples.

I personally have seen paralyzed, deaf, blind, and broken bodies totally healed.

In His last prayer on Earth, Jesus prayed for all who would come after His disciples, saying, *"And I ask not only for these disciples, but also for all those who will one day believe in me through their message"* (John 17:20 TPT). Our believing in the message of Jesus gives us access to His love, salvation, and power. It's still for today! He's still moving in a mighty way across this earth. Don't let anyone tell you that the age of healing is over. Someone might say, "Well, we don't see the amount of miracles that Jesus had in His ministry though." Perhaps it is we who have taken the step back from Him. Through reliance on modern medicine and readily available natural solutions, the Westernized church has grown complacent. In other regions of the world where there is little healthcare, creative miracles and supernatural healings are very much a common thing.

Carrying Healing to Others

Not only can we receive healing for ourselves, but also we can pray for others to be healed. We are jars of clay that carry the Holy Spirit wherever we go. Jesus commanded us to carry healing to others. Luke 10:9 (TPT) says, *"Heal the sick, and tell them all, 'God's kingdom realm has arrived and is now within your reach!'"* We have the same healing anointing available to us that Jesus operated in. We are told to pray for the sick and to lay hands on them in faith. James 5:16b says, *"Pray one for another that you may be healed."*

So let me ask you a question: **<u>Would God tell you to pray for something that is outside of His will?</u>**

James 5:14-15a say:

> *Is anyone among you sick? Let them call the elders of the church to pray over them and anoint them with oil in the name of the Lord. And the prayer offered in faith **will make the sick person well; the Lord will raise them up**.*

Again, would God tell us to do something that is not His will? Would He promise, "They will be healed" if He didn't mean it? Would He tell His kids to do something that was not His view of what was right? NO! His will is to heal all who are oppressed (Acts 10:38).

However, just like when Jesus couldn't do many miracles due to His hometown's dishonor and unbelief, we cannot heal people arbitrarily. We have no power without God. We either must hear the Holy Spirit's leading to operate in the gifts of healing, or we need to locate that person's faith by asking if they believe Jesus already paid for their healing on the cross. They must put a draw on the anointing or be open to receiving. Often, people who are sick are desperate for any help or answers, so it's a great time to share the Truth with them. They are usually open to an answer because pain is no fun! Sharing a testimony like mine produces hope, and then teaching them the Word produces faith.

When I pray for people, I first ask them if they believe Jesus has already provided for their healing, and then I say, "Well then, I come into agreement with YOUR faith." Often as I pray for people, the Lord reveals some blockages to them receiving healing, such as an identity issue or an unforgiveness issue. It's important to share with them what the Holy Spirit is saying with them, because they are the only ones who can allow the Lord into that place in their heart.

By the way, just because someone you prayed for didn't get healed, don't create a doctrine that God doesn't heal. Instead, continue to help them understand the principles you've learned. Get the Word of God to them so they can grow their own faith.

Knowing God's Will

So, can we know God's will concerning healing? Yes. How? One way is through seeing the example of Jesus and what He did about sickness. Another way is through revelation by the Spirit of God that is inside of us:

> But as it is written: "Eye has not seen, nor ear heard, nor have entered into the heart of man the things which God has prepared for those who love Him." But God has revealed them to us through His Spirit. For the Spirit searches all things, yes, the deep things of God. For what man knows the things of a man except the spirit of the man which is in him? Even so no one knows the things of God except the Spirit of God. Now we have received, not the spirit of the world, but the Spirit who is from God, that we might know the things that have been freely given to us by God. These things we also speak, not in words which man's wisdom teaches but which the Holy Spirit teaches, comparing spiritual things with spiritual.
>
> —1 Corinthians 2:9-13 (NKJV)

The Holy Spirit reveals God's will to us by leading us with peace. His still, small voice of revelation feels like peace inside of our hearts.

When we read the Truth, He affirms it. He speaks clearly when we have trained our hearts to listen and hear.

I hope you are convinced and confident that you can trust God's character and you can know God's will. All of the arguments of men mean nothing when you have the evidence of your faith! Someone can tell me all day long that God doesn't heal, that it's not His will, but it's too late! I'm not going to believe them. I've already been healed! And you just can't argue with evidence.

 **READ**

Matthew 8:14-17

 DETOX:

Have you been told it's not God's will to heal? Do you now have peace in reading all of the scriptural evidence I've been laying out concerning healing?

 SELF-REFLECTION:

What are some things you know are changing in your mind-set or in your life as you are going through this study? Give God praise and thanks for what He is doing!

TODAY'S TAKEAWAY:

Jesus revealed that it's Father God's will to heal all who believe.

PRAYER

Lord, You said that You constantly think good thoughts toward me. You are kind and merciful. I rejoice in You, so happy and thankful that You are my Father—the best Father ever! And I can know Your will for every situation of my life. Thank You for revealing Your plans, desires, and will to me. Amen.

Day
22

STAND IN AUTHORITY
THE LION
OF JUDAH

DAY 22

My friend Annamarie was in the fight of her life. She had gone from being a joyful person to plunging into deep postpartum depression after the birth of her second child. She was battling extreme bouts of anxiety, lack of connection with her baby, and even suicidal thoughts. Her beautiful singing even suffered, because she felt like she couldn't hear notes.

She had lost her confidence. The devil kept telling her that she was going crazy, that she was going to hell, and that God was far away. All she could do was remind herself of what she had been taught and that she had indeed made Jesus the Lord of her life, even though her emotions felt so tormented.

I remember praying with her many times and feeling so angry at the devil because of what she was going through. It's terrible to have someone you love suffer.

But through that, I realized that the best thing we can do for those who are struggling is to encourage them with the Truth, show them lots of unconditional love, listen to them, and pray for them.

If you know someone who is struggling, don't be afraid to get into the trenches with them. There are many times in life when we need a friend, spouse, mentor, or pastor to come alongside of us and help us stand. Annamarie and her wonderful husband did a great job of surrounding themselves with several people they could call for prayer and encouragement.

If you feel like you are weak and cannot stand on your own, please reach out to people who know the Word of God! It's okay to tell someone that you're not okay. It's okay to ask for help. It's often through the encouragement of the family of God that we find the strength and the courage to not surrender and to get back in the fight.

After going to the doctor, Annamarie was also diagnosed with hypo-thyroidism, put on medication, and told, "You will be on this for the rest of your life."

After getting on the medication, things got slightly better physically, but mentally and emotionally, it was a fight just to function. You might understand. You might have fought the same torment. Or maybe you still are fighting.

Right in the middle of that season, God gave Annamarie a song. Maybe you've heard it from our worship band, Open Heaven. It's called "Lion of Judah," and you HAVE to look it up! The powerful lyrics say:

> I know you hear my cry;
> You even know my thoughts.
> You're present in everything, my King,
> The Lion of Judah.
> I see You in mountains high.
> I hear You when oceans roar.
> You cry out Your love for me, My King,
> The Lion of Judah.
> So Lion of Judah, roar!
> We won't be silent anymore.
> Lion of Judah, roar!

> Mighty battle cry, come forth!
> I can see the mountains. They tremble
> At the sound of Your name.
> I can hear the sounds of revival
> Shaking this place.
> I can feel the winds of Your Spirit
> Breaking every chain.
> I can hear the cries of Your people singing.

As she wrote it, she had a picture of Jesus, represented by a mighty lion like Aslan in the *Chronicles of Narnia,* roaring behind her. He was defending her and challenging all who tried to oppress her. This was a song of deliverance, and God gave it to her to remind her that *He* was fighting for her. But she, too, had to stand up and fight.

Now, understand that Annamarie is a sweet Southern girl who wouldn't harm a fly, and she's not a fighter by nature, but she realized she was at war.

As she had this realization, something happened. Annamarie made a decision that would change everything. Let me share in her own words:

> My breakthrough came when I learned to fight in the Spirit. I realized that I wasn't crazy; I was under attack. I stopped feeling sorry for myself and started fighting by faith. <u>I made a decision to win</u>. I can honestly say my breakthrough with depression and my thyroid came because I made the decision that I wasn't going to be on medication my whole life. I wasn't going to partake in generational curses (both depres-

sion and thyroid disease are generational curses in my family). I decided to trust God and say yes to His promises. <u>I stopped fighting in the flesh and stepped into faith.</u>

When Annamarie did that, everything changed! Those bouts of severe anxiety and depression started subsiding. They didn't disappear instantly, because the devil would come back every once in a while to see if she still believed God's Word, but she got stronger and stronger. She could think clearly once again. She found joy.

And then she became convinced that she did not need the medication anymore, so she saw her doctor, had the necessary tests, and got the results. Somewhat baffled, her doctor confirmed that she no longer needed to take any more thyroid medication whatsoever! What once was a lifelong prognosis had disappeared. It was a miracle! But really, her deliverance and healing were the fruit of her faith, a totally normal occurrence in the Kingdom of God.

Since then, she has had two more children, and she had no post partum depression with either. She is writing songs and leading worship again. God has restored what the enemy tried to steal, and through Him, she has broken generational curses. It stopped with her, and she's not going back!

I want to remind you that if you are battling anxiety and depression, just like Annamarie was, or you find yourself in the fight of your life, there is One who is able, and He is on your side!

Then one of the elders said to me, "Do not weep! See, the Lion of the tribe of Judah, the Root of David, has triumphed. He is able to open the scroll and its seven seals."

—Revelation 5:5

Jesus has already defeated the spirits of depression and anxiety. He has come to restore your confidence. He wants you to get your fight back! And you don't have to fight this battle in your own strength. In fact, none of us are able to live this life on our own merit, talent, willpower, or might. We must rely on He who is able to move heaven and Earth on our behalves!

He is roaring over you, defending you, and protecting you from all adversaries. Now, it's YOUR time to rise up in His might and His power and to boldly proclaim His Word. When you speak His Word under the power of the Holy Spirit, the devil thinks it's Jesus speaking! Why? Because He gave you His Spirit, anointing, and AUTHORITY.

Jesus said, in John 14:

> *"I tell you this timeless truth: The person who follows me in faith, believing in me, will do the same mighty miracles that I do— even greater miracles than these because I go to be with my Father! For I will do whatever you ask me to do when you ask me in my name. And that is how the Son will show what the Father is really like and bring glory to him. <u>Ask me anything in my name, and I will do it for you!</u>"*

—John 14:12-14 (TPT)

The Greek translation of that very last phrase, "and I will do it for you," is much stronger and more emphatic than what English can convey.

It literally means, "If you ask anything in my name, <u>if I don't have it, I'll make it for you.</u>"

That reminds me of when we would visit my Grandma's house down south several times a year. Grandma is a great Southern cook, and she would ask us, "What do you want me to make for you?"

She would make me my favorite pound cake and make my brother his favorite peanut butter fudge. Every year as a Christmas present, she still makes us each a by-request meal at her house.

Just like she desires to bless us, God has the desire to bless His kids—so much so that He will create new paths, new positions, and new body parts (whatever we ask for in His name) to bring Him glory!

Let's not diminish God's power by asking for little or believing for nothing.

Many of us have unemployed angels just sitting around hoping we will speak some faith so they can get to work on our behalves! Many of us have unbelievers around us watching to see if what we believe actually works. Some of us have segments of society we are called to reach, and those people in those areas are just waiting for someone who is different, who has hope, and who has peace because they have answers.

Friend, it's time we Christians take back our authority and start living revolutionary lives like Jesus did!

Hebrews 10:38 says, *"But my righteous one will live by faith. And <u>I</u>*

take no pleasure in the one who shrinks back."

We can't change the world or change someone else's life until we stop shrinking back in the shadows, allowing the power and authority Jesus gave us to sit dormant.

Because she was willing to rise up and fight, Annamarie's songs she's written since that time have impacted many people. But what if she had allowed the enemy to steal her song? What if she had remained in that place of low confidence? Others would have never been set free through those songs of deliverance.

Remember, you are going to have bad days during which problems and circumstances come knocking. That's when you must run to Jesus, keep yourself in a place of peace, and remind yourself that God is always able.

The Great Physician is on our side. He heals our wounds, He restores our fortunes, and He fights our battles for us. He's the Lion of the Tribe of Judah!

Sure, life isn't always a walk in the park. It's war sometimes, because we are taking territory for Jesus until He returns, and we live in enemy-held territory. But... the documents of surrender have already been signed and sealed, and now we are just breaking down the enemy's encampments, freeing those who are held captive, and letting them know that THE WAR IS OVER!

And guess what? WE ALREADY WON!

 **READ**

Romans 6:4, Acts 3:1-10

 # DETOX:

Do any of Annamarie's thoughts or symptoms sound familiar? Have you surrendered to them instead of standing?

 # SELF-REFLECTION:

How are you applying the Truth you are learning so far? Do you feel that your faith muscles have grown since starting this 30-day Healing Dare? What was your biggest takeaway from Annamarie's story?

 # TODAY'S TAKEAWAY:

I am bold and confident because the Lion of the Tribe of Judah is fighting for me. I resist fear, anxiety, and depression with the power of His name! (To hear the song "Lion of Judah," find Open Heaven Band on all streaming platforms or go to OpenHeavenBand.com.)

PRAYER

Jesus, help me not to pull back in fear, but help me to stand in authority, which comes from You alone. Draw me closer to You as You roar over me. I rebuke the spirits of anxiety and depression, in the name of Jesus! If Annamarie was set free, I can be too! You are no respecter of persons, and You don't play favorites. I receive Your deliverance now from anything that has been oppressing me, in the powerful name of Jesus! Amen!

STAND IN AUTHORITY

THE DAY
OF TROUBLE

W hat happens when an unexpected attack comes? Everything seems to be going fine, then perhaps we let down our guard, and, suddenly, we find ourselves being bombarded with opportunities to let go of our faith. We have a really, really bad day. It's then that we have a life-or-death choice: stand in faith or give in to fear.

Adam faced just that, an attack that should have taken him out. I want to share his story through the perspective of his wife, Connie, who became a spiritual warrior fighting for her husband during this time.

Adam's Story

Adam was driving home on the night of June 15 when he saw headlights in front of him in his lane. Before he had time to react, a drunk driver struck him going 65 mph. He blacked out. The next thing he knew was someone was at his window telling him he had to get out because his car was on fire. But the door was jammed.

Adam doesn't remember how, but he climbed through his crumpled car and exited through a back window. This was miraculous in itself, because they would later find out Adam had broken his right hip socket, left ankle, right elbow, left wrist, and he had 24 fractures in his face, nose, and palate.

As he was placed in the ambulance, all he could whisper was, "Jesus." He said it over and over to himself. When he arrived at the hospital, the doctor declared him in critical condition and asked him if he needed to talk to a chaplain. Adam was able to give his wife's number to the chaplain, who then called Connie.

The night before the accident, Connie could not sleep. She tossed and turned and then got up to pray. She prayed until 5:30 a.m. and told her husband that day, "I guess someone really needed prayer."

When she last talked to Adam on the phone and they said goodbye before hanging up, she said out loud, "That felt weird."

When she pulled into her driveway later that night, Adam wasn't home. It was an hour past when he was supposed to get home, and he was never late. She then saw images in her spirit of a car accident, so she started to pray.

When a call came in from an unknown number a few minutes later, her first words were, "Is he alive?" It was the chaplain, who told her that Adam was in critical condition and she needed to come right away.

Connie says:

> "I declared IMMEDIATELY that Adam would live and not die and would declare the works of the Lord. Those were the first words that came out of my mouth when I called the first few people. I told them they were to say NOTHING other than those words, and they could pray Psalm 91. Even when I called Adam's mom, I was obviously crying but only spoke those words and told her to speak nothing else to his siblings. I also told her that if she did call them and they decided to come, they were to say nothing negative or they would be asked to leave."

Connie's emotions and body were obviously reacting, as you can imagine, but inside of her a fight rose up. She had spent all night long praying in the Spirit, and little did she know that she was arming herself for the fight. She says, "This was an illegal event, and the enemy didn't have a chance."

When she got to the hospital, she immediately started setting the atmosphere in his room. She says:

> "I asked doctors to only speak life over him and anything else to tell me in private. They couldn't plant any seeds of doubt into his subconscious. When people came to visit and were declaring the Word over Adam, they had more time with him. When people came in needing to mourn or grieve in front of us, basically needing me to comfort them, they were asked to leave with a five-minute time limit. I even had to kick out a family member! I also told everyone that came to visit (even siblings and parents) that they were not to cry in the room with him and to only speak positive words.

> When Adam woke up, we still did not chat with doctors regarding his prognosis in front of him. Doctors did not have great things to say, but I came back into the room and declared, 'We will be out by Thursday!'

> Doctors were talking about weeks, and I spoke in terms of days. We were always taught by your family that we get what we speak and that our words are seeds from which we get the fruit. And that is exactly what we got."

Friends came to pray in the waiting room over the next week, bringing Scriptures written on cards and posting photos of a healed and whole Adam on his hospital room walls.

On June 22, Adam was allowed to go home from the hospital. He came back a few days later for surgery but was released for the final time on June 30—just 15 days after what should have been a fatal car accident! It was a miraculous recovery in every way.

On August 10, he was released to start walking with a walker—only he never used the walker! Haha!

Today, Adam is better than ever. He is stronger physically. One year after being hit at 65 mph, he ran a 5K! Today, he jogs consistently, plays basketball weekly, and enjoys life thoroughly.

He has also found a new perspective, free from stress, because he knows what really matters—love, joy, and peace.

Connie says, "The main thing has become the main thing. For example, prior to the accident there was this sense of 'one day, we will _____ (go on trips, find a less stressful job...).'" Now they take advantage of every opportunity and every moment together.

When Connie talked to the police officer who responded to the 911 call, he told her that when they walked up to his burning car, they fully expected for whoever was in there to be deceased. "We don't know how he climbed out of that car," he told Connie. "He is very lucky."

Connie replied, "No, he has a big God."

That reminds me of this verse:

> *Jesus looked at them and said, "With man this is impossible, but with God all things are possible."*
> —Matthew 19:26

Adam and Connie stood on the Word, and what should have been fatal—or at the very least, months or years of recovery—became just two weeks in the hospital and a short recovery at home.

So how did Connie overcome when that day of trouble came? Having attended our church, she had heard story after story of how God healed, delivered, restored, and saved. Connie shares that's what helped her the most:

"The biggest thing that helped me was having heard all the stories before mine, and knowing their outcome. God saved him [Adam], but the stories saved him. I knew immediately that if God saved XYZ, then He would save Adam. I knew real-life examples before my situation happened. I knew what Scripture to stand on when emotions were real and in my face. We surrounded ourselves with the Word and knew our picture —Adam's healthy body. We knew our authority. Even in a demon-filled hospital, we have authority where we step. That room belonged to us (because we were paying for it.) Those doctors and nurses could not help but speak life, because they walked into an encounter with the Holy Spirit. One thing I would recommend to anyone dealing with a trauma, especially if they are being the caretaker, is to continue in daily alone time, so that their identity doesn't become 'caretaker' but stays 'son' or 'daughter' of God."

Connie and Adam are living, breathing examples of this promise from God: "*...and call on me in the day of trouble; I will deliver you, and you will honor me*" (Psalm 50:15).

Preparing for Battle

So what should we do before a potential battle ever comes? Connie gave us some really great suggestions.

All of those suggestions can be summarized in what the Bible calls "putting on the full armor of God."

It's called armor because it will protect you, even in unexpected attacks.

Ephesians 6:10-18 say:

> *Finally, be strong in the Lord and in his mighty power. Put on the full armor of God, so that you can <u>take your stand against the devil's schemes</u>. For our struggle is not against flesh and blood, but against the rulers, against the authorities, against the powers of this dark world and against the spiritual forces of evil in the heavenly realms.*
>
> *<u>Therefore put on the full armor of God, so that when the day of evil comes, you may be able to stand your ground</u>, and after you have done everything, to stand. Stand firm then, with the belt of truth buckled around your waist, with the breastplate of righteousness in place, and with your feet fitted with the readiness that comes from the gospel of peace. In addition to all this,*

take up the shield of faith, with which you can extinguish all the flaming arrows of the evil one. Take the helmet of salvation and the sword of the Spirit, which is the word of God. And pray in the Spirit on all occasions with all kinds of prayers and requests. With this in mind, be alert and always keep on praying for all the Lord's people.

The right preparation and tools are key to having victory in every situation:

- Have you ever been in the hot sun all day without sunscreen?
- Have you ever gone into a store without money?
- Have you ever taken a test in class that you weren't prepared to take?

That reminds me of my first time skiing. My family and I were in Whistler, Alberta, Canada. It was summertime, and my mom decided we were going skiing. Now, we had never tried it, and as we rented gear, we found out there was only one slope open—a black diamond slope on the very top of the mountain where the glacier ice never melts.

We didn't even know what "black diamond" meant! Haha!

As we rode four chair lifts to an elevation of 10,000 feet, my heart nearly stopped. Guess who else was on that mountain? None other than the U.S. Olympic ski team!

I was not prepared for this moment. I had never taken a lesson. I didn't know how to use any of the equipment. I didn't even know how to stand up without falling!

When my mom and I had finally fallen all the way down the glacier, stopping just short of the jagged rocks at the bottom and certain death, it was only then that we realized we had to ride a tow rope back up the glacier.

If you don't know, a tow rope is a bar you put behind your back and you hold onto as it propels you up. But you still have to ski, and you have to know how to steer.

It was the only way out of there.

We did okay for the first 20 feet. Then the tow rope hit an incline that felt like we were lying on our backs, looking straight up at the sky. That's when my mom slipped over on top of me and she literally rode me up the rest of the way, like a sled!

We slid side to side precariously. I realized that if we let go, we would hit every skier riding up behind us. But if we didn't let go, we were about to crash into huge rocks on either side of us.

The people at the top were yelling, "Let go! Let go!" The people behind us were yelling, "Don't let go! Don't let go!"

In a split decision, mom made a leap for the rocks and I followed, grabbing hold of them while they stopped the entire tow rope operation and sent guys on jet skis to rescue us.

I think my embarrassment was worse than the cuts and bruises I sustained. Let's just say my first skiing experience was a massive disaster. I was not prepared!

In the same way, many of us do not prepare for battle until we are in the foxhole with shells dropping around us. While satan's weapons are no match for God's weapons, most Christians have not learned how to pick up God's weapons and prepare for warfare.

Connie and Adam had prepared their spirits for warfare by attending a church that let them hear about God's faithfulness to others, taught them the Word, and encouraged them in their authority. They had godly friends around them. They studied their rights. They put on the armor of God.

Remember when Connie said she had prayed in the Spirit the entire night before? She was doing what Paul said: "*And pray in the Spirit on all occasions with all kinds of prayers and requests.*" (Ephesians 6:18a).

Again, let me encourage you that satan's attacks have absolutely no power over us unless we give him our authority with words of doubt and unbelief. Satan is holding a banana gun, while God's weapons are like tanks and AK-47 assault rifles. It's no contest!

But you need to learn how to operate that tank and enforce your victory.

The enemy has been defeated. It's a done deal. Now stand! Put a demand on the Kingdom inside of you! We have been given the same power Jesus had, through the Holy Spirit inside of us, to absolutely turn things right side up. When we know who we are in Christ (identity), and we have faith in God (belief), plus we take action and speak with authority (legal enforcement), we are going to see the same results that Jesus saw. He healed the sick, cast out demons, changed hearts, confronted evil, spoke the Truth, and inspired people to spread the Gospel all over the world!

We do not have to fear calamity or disaster. We do not have to be unprepared for the day of battle. Our hearts can rest in the might of the Lord. Psalm 112:7 says, "*They will have no fear of bad news; their hearts are steadfast, trusting in the Lord.*"

Stuff happens sometimes because we live in occupied territory, in a fallen world filled with sinful people, and we have an adversary. There are going to be battles. There are going to be bad days. Jesus said that in this life we will have trouble, but to be of good cheer because He has overcome the world (John 16:33).

King David's Bad Day

We all have challenges because we live in a fallen world. We have people around us who are being influenced by the enemy, and we have to learn how to deal with these obstacles in a godly way. So what do we do when we have a really bad day? King David was faced with one when he and his army came back from a winning battle, only to then be faced with the most devastating situation of their lives. First Samuel 30:3-4 say:

When David and his men reached Ziklag, they found it destroyed by fire and their wives and sons and daughters taken captive. So David and his men wept aloud until they had no strength left to weep.

Their entire lives were gone. Wives and kids, gone. Homes and possessions, burned. Then David's men wanted to stone him because in their grief they wanted someone to blame, and the leader is an easy target. There was nothing but devastation and grief all around David.

What did David do? Well, he didn't know *what* to do in his own strength, so he inquired of the Lord. He didn't rely on his own logic, military experience, or assumptions. He didn't succumb to his own grief. He stood up and led his men to the throne room of God. As he prayed, God told him to pursue the enemy and told him that he would be successful in his pursuit. So David and 400 of his men left, caught up to the enemy, and with God's help, defeated ALL of the soldiers there. It took two days of fighting. But they were victorious! Though they were outnumbered, God was on David's side.

Verses 18-19 say,

David recovered everything the Amalekites had taken, including his two wives. <u>Nothing was missing</u>: young or old, boy or girl, plunder or anything else they had taken. David brought everything back.

All was restored. They plundered the enemy's camp and took back all the provisions needed to rebuild and then some. Not one of their family members was harmed. On the day of evil, in a fight for his life,

David turned to God and followed His guidance.

One day, all of the sorrow and devastation of this world will end. No more earthly sorrow. No more discouraging events happening around us. No more living in this war zone called Earth. We will enjoy our heavenly reward! And there's a day coming when God is going to lock up that serpent, the ancient liar, and throw him into a fiery prison forever and ever. God will wipe every tear from our eyes. But until that Glorious Day, we are called to <u>occupy till He comes</u> (Luke 19:13, KJV). Just know that God is there, leading you and giving you the victory, even on the worst day of your life. It can become the greatest victory you've ever seen. It can become a day of restoration and redemption. It can become the pivot point upon which you build the rest of your life. Your setback can be a setup for victory!

† READ

Go back through Ephesians 6:10-18, and say them out loud in first person. Also, read Hebrews 11:6.

DETOX:

In what area do you feel least prepared for battle? What could you eliminate from your life in order to allow more time to "put on your armor" everyday? (That means reading the Bible, worshipping God, praying in the Holy Spirit, listening to teachings, and speaking life over yourself.)

SELF-REFLECTION:

What's the hardest thing you've ever faced? Were you prepared? How could you have prepared yourself spiritually in a greater way for that battle? Is there anything you would do differently now, in light of Connie and Adam's story?

 # TODAY'S TAKEAWAY:

Today, I stand with my spiritual armor on, and I know that in every situation I have the victory Jesus won for me.

PRAYER

Lord, I put on Your full armor today so that I can stand!

- *I put on the helmet of salvation, which assures me that any thoughts from the devil just bounce right off of the sanctified mind of Christ that I now possess.*

- *I am surrounded by Truth, the belt of Truth, and I refuse to take it off.*

- *I put on the breastplate of righteousness, which protects my heart from attacks against my identity and from condemnation or shame. I am righteous!*

- *My feet are ready to take the Gospel of peace to this world. And I choose to walk in peace only. I refuse to step in the way of fear.*

- *I lift up my shield of faith, a defense against every attack. My faith extinguishes doubt, emotional turmoil, and every evil weapon.*

- *I wield my Spirit sword, the Bible, which puts to death every lie and cuts off the head of every thought that doesn't line up with the Truth. Your Word is a weapon that divides what is right from what is wrong.*

- *And I commit to pray more in the Holy Spirit and speak in my heavenly language.*

STAND IN AUTHORITY

BOLD AND COURAGEOUS

F riend, it's time to take back your courage and stand in your authority! That's what I had to learn how to do when I was sick.

You see, I knew *God* was able, but I didn't think *I* was able. I doubted *my* strength. But that's when I had to just start believing that this Scripture applied to me too: *"I can do all this through him who gives me strength"* (Philippians 4:13).

We may be walking in the devil's streets, or what the Bible calls "the Valley of the Shadow of Death," but we don't have to fear any evil, because our Daddy God is bigger and stronger than any evil, and He is with us!

Even though the devil has jurisdiction in this world to tempt us to step out of faith, we can use an authority that is higher than him. He wants to steal, kill, and destroy, but everywhere we go, we can bring abundant life through Jesus's power at work within us. We are not on the defense; we are on the offense! We can introduce God into every circumstance, much like a physician can introduce an antibiotic into a body to kill an infection. **Have a problem? Give it a good dose of God! We can bring His power into the streets where we walk.** If we get into a jam, we can call for backup! Heaven's armies will fight for us to protect us in all we do!

Why do we lose courage? Because we turn away from the mirror of the Word of God and start forgetting who we are. But when we continually expose our spirits to the love of God and the picture of hope found in His Word, our spirits thrive and our confidence grows.

No matter what the doctor's report says or what the devil has told you, no sickness or disease can triumph against God's power in you! The devil has no right to take you out before it's time. You belong to the land of the healthy and the living. You belong here!

Sure, there will be voices that try to shush your faith—voices of doubt that will try to convince you that you don't have a place at the table of God. That's when you have a choice that needs made often throughout the day: Whose voice are you going to listen to?

I hope you've already made a decision to listen to our Father, to believe what He says *about* you in order to receive what He has already given *to* you.

What Courage Looks Like

Remember the story I told in the beginning about Rikki being healed of those impossible, baseball-sized fibroid tumors? Rikki's tenacious belief in God's ability and her stubborn refusal to pay attention to the fearful thoughts that kept trying to come resulted in a cancelled surgery and a healed body. When she focused all of her attention on God's Word, it completely eliminated the problem! She was healed overnight, just as I was.

Remember Annamarie? She had to get tough on that spirit of depression and allow the Lion of Judah to roar through her over her circumstances. She spoke to the "storm" with authority, and it stopped.

Connie had to stand like a warrior for her husband, not in her own strength but in the strength of the Holy Spirit, and put on the armor of God. She refused to relent. She would not let go of God's promise over Adam's life, and he is a walking miracle today.

What do courage and confidence look like? I picture a lighthouse, standing on the edge of tumultuous waters, standing tall and bright in the middle of the night, though lashed by waves and storms. It doesn't waver or shake. It simply stands. In the same way, we can simply stand, courageous in the face of wind and waves. We can shine in the darkest night through the light of God's love in our hearts. That lighthouse speaks of strength, safety, and comfort to any sailor who is lost at sea. In the same way, our faith speaks strength, safety, and comfort even smack dab in the middle of the worst season of our lives. We must stand up to the bullying tactics of the enemy, SPEAK, and command him to leave.

In the story found in Mark 4, Jesus was stuck in a boat, lost in a storm in the middle of the Sea of Galilee with a bunch of fearful sailors. They were freaking out and telling Jesus that they were all going to die. The storm must have been pretty fierce to scare the most hardened of sailors who grew up on the water.

Yet, Jesus was unmoved. In fact, he took on a scolding tone with His disciples and took them to task for their lack of faith. They thought they were going to die, and Jesus was treating this like it was no big deal. **His faith dictated His future.** He was unmoved. He simply stepped up, commanded the storm to stop, and it did. *"He got up, rebuked the wind and said to the waves, 'Quiet! Be still!' Then the wind died down and it was completely calm"* (Mark 4:39).

He took courage when others took fear. But how? It's easy to say we have courage until we see a life-threatening situation. Well, Jesus *knew* that He *knew* that He *knew* where He was going, who He was, and what His Father was capable of doing for Him. We can be too. In fact, that's what Jesus expected out of His disciples, who had seen Him do so many astounding miracles. They disappointed Him that day, but they eventually learned how to trust and stand up, even in the midst of the storms of life.

When I learned this principle of taking my authority and standing in courage, I started doing little marches around my house or drives around the countryside during which I would speak to my problems about God. I would command the storm to stop. I would rebuke the devil and demand that he leave. I would speak the Word of God as loudly as I could—the volume wasn't so that God could hear me (He's not deaf), but because it made me feel more confident. Hearing my own tone of authority gave me courage. My mind, will, and emotions needed to hear confidence, even if it was coming from my own mouth—especially coming from my own mouth!

A while back I found myself fighting a bad virus, and it just wouldn't seem to go away. I was in bed for two weeks! The fatigue was crazy. Then I realized that even though I had been speaking the Word, I had not commanded that evil thing to leave my body *with authority*. So I listened to some healing teaching, got out of bed, and started pacing my bedroom. At first, I spoke quietly, walked slowly, and commanded that evil virus to wither and die. But then I gained strength and courage until I was pacing furiously and speaking loudly. From that very moment, I started to recover quickly. I was back on my feet and playing outside with the kids within two days. None of my kids nor my husband caught it. We cut it off from our family. The fight was over the moment I got myself up and took back my authority. I stopped giving that virus authority to harm my body. I started giving God legal access to my life, and He healed me. I had no remaining side effects.

My friend Brittany found herself in the hospital with a terrible disease that was literally sapping the nourishment out of her body. She is one of the strongest people I know, and most people who know her call her Wonder Woman. But at that moment in her life, it didn't look good. Then she discovered a key:

> From me, growing up in a Christian home all my life, I believed that I was healed, but I never really decided to confess it out loud. My husband and I decided to come into agreement about some things in our household, and IMMEDIATELY, things started to change! A few more months went by, and I began to hear more stories from other church members about them receiving their healings and lives being changed. What I noticed was that they all had one thing in common: They verbalized their outcomes! One night, I made a conscious decision to do just that!

She stood up and refused to bow to the enemy's attempts on her life. She took her authority and spoke the Word. Even in her worst moment, still extremely frail and hospitalized, she spoke life. When I visited her in the hospital, I smiled when I saw what was sitting on her bedside table. It was a pair of very sparkly high heels. She told me, "That's my reminder that I'm walking out of here! The enemy CANNOT take me out. I'm coming through this." She made a courageous decision to stand up to the problem. She would live and not die and would declare the works of the Lord. Here's what happened:

> I was awakened in the middle of the night and began to feel this tug on my stomach. At first, I thought it was another episode of cramps, but I heard the Holy Spirit repeatedly say to me "Open your eyes, open your eyes." As soon as I did, I felt this huge pull, like a bandage coming off my stomach, and I could see this cloud leave my body. I knew right then and there that I was completely healed! I know that my God is a healer, and all we have to do is learn how to confess (verbalize) with our mouths that HE is Lord and have faith (agree with HIS Kingdom). HE will do the rest!

Sure enough, she is healed and whole today. In fact, she gave birth to twins several years after being at death's door! She calls them her double portion twins, because God gave her double for her trouble!

For this last day on the topic of standing in authority, I want you to read each of the following promises out loud, followed by a confession of your faith based on that promise. Do it as many times as needed until you feel your courage renewed!

Scriptures on Courage and Confidence:

God's Promise: *"Let us hold unswervingly to the hope we profess, for he who promised is faithful"* (Hebrews 10:23).

Your Confession: I refuse to back down from this hope, and I know the God who made me these promises is faithful.

God's Promise: *"For the Lord will be your confidence and will keep your foot from being caught"* (Proverbs 3:26, ESV).
Your Confession: I am confident in my God, because He will keep my foot from being caught.

God's Promise: *"Don't be afraid, for I am with you. Don't be discouraged, for I am your God. I will strengthen you and help you. I will hold you up with my victorious right hand"* (Isaiah 41:10, NLT).
Your Confession: I will not be afraid for God is with me. I won't be discouraged for God is my Father.

God's Promise: *"For the Lord your God will be with you, wherever you go"* (Joshua 1:9b).
Your Confession: The Lord my God is with me wherever I go.

God's Promise: *"Receive this truth: Whatever you forbid on earth will be considered to be forbidden in heaven, and whatever you release on earth will be considered to be released in heaven. Again, I give you an eternal truth: If two of you agree to ask God for something in a symphony of prayer, my heavenly Father will do it for you. For wherever two or three come together in honor of my name, I am right there with them"* (Matthew 18:18-20, TPT)!
Your Confession: I receive the Truth that I can forbid something on Earth and heaven will back me up. I can release something on the Earth, and heaven will back me up. If I come into agreement with someone in faith, it will be done for me. God is right here in the midst of us!

God's Promise: *"Jesus summoned together his twelve apostles and imparted to them authority over every demon and the power to heal every disease. Then he commissioned them to preach God's kingdom realm and to <u>heal the sick</u> to demonstrate that the kingdom had arrived"* (Luke 9:1-2a, TPT).

Your Confession: Jesus has given me authority over every demon and the power to heal the sick, because I am His disciple. I can preach God's Kingdom and heal the sick to demonstrate that the Kingdom is real!

God's Promise: *"Now you understand that I have imparted to you all my authority to trample over his kingdom. You will trample upon every demon before you and overcome every power Satan possesses. <u>Absolutely nothing will be able to harm you as you walk in this authority</u>. However, your real source of joy isn't merely that these spirits submit to your authority, but that your names are written in the journals of heaven and that you belong to God's kingdom. This is the true source of your authority"* (Luke 10:19-20 TPT).

Your Confession: I have authority to trample on every demon and to overcome every power of the enemy. Nothing will harm me! I walk in authority. And I celebrate God's promise that my name is written in His book because I belong to Him.

God's Promise: *"And this is the confidence that we have in him, that if we ask anything according to his will, he heareth us: And if we know that he hears us, whatsoever we ask, we know that we have the petitions that we desired of him"* (1 John 5:14-15, KJV).

Your Confession: I am confident because if I ask anything that's God's will, He hears me, and I have what I've asked.

DETOX:

What's one thing you say about yourself that you now know doesn't line up with God's picture of boldness and courage? Write it down and then *cross it out*. Commit to eliminate it from this day forward.

 ## SELF-REFLECTION:

Health is one of God's promises to you. Have you stood on that and put on the full armor of God? Or have you let doubts and circumstances steal your confidence? What's one promise you are going to repeat daily concerning your authority and your confidence in God?

 ## TODAY'S TAKEAWAY:

I will be bold and courageous because I can trust God's promises to me. He does not lie!

TESTIMONY:

"The message you gave Sunday really helped me! I just recently had major knee surgery and was told that I wouldn't return to normal for at least six to eight months. Thanks to the message given Sunday, I now thank God that I am able to do everything normally and that I'm free of pain."

—Veronica F.

PRAYER

Jesus, today I stand in agreement with your Word that says, "By Your stripes, I was healed." I am the healed of the Lord! Your goodness sustains me, and I will have no fear. I am confident in You. I am fully persuaded that faith works every time. I will not be shaken! I will not be moved off of this Truth!

THE PRAYER OF FAITH

AGREEMENT WITH GOD

W e have been working through the five keys that God taught me in order to receive my healing. They are principles from His Word that will work for anyone, just like a car can be driven by anyone who knows how to operate one. Let's review the ones we have already studied, and let's add in a new one for today's reading:

1. Reclaim your identity. (Know who you are in Christ.)

2. Repaint your picture. (Faith is being fully persuaded of God's promises.)

3. Stand in your authority (Enforce the victory with courage, and speak your desired outcome.)

4. Pray the prayer of faith when you are fully persuaded. (NEW one! Let's chat about this.)

Faith of a Child

"Mom, I sowed a seed for a dog at church today," my sister Kirsten, then 13, told my mom. She showed my mom a picture of a Pomeranian puppy on her wall.

Dad and Mom were not super excited about another dog, so they gave Kirsten a stuffed Pomeranian toy for Christmas. But that only helped Kirsten's picture. She held fast to the fact that when she prayed, she believed she had received that Pomeranian puppy, so her faith said she had it.

Despite Dad telling her, "Kirsten, we don't want another dog in the house," she simply replied, "Mom says God can change the heart of the king." Haha! Smart!

Soon after, my parents had a ministry trip during which they preached at a church. The pastor came up to them after the service and said, "It's the strangest thing. I breed Pomeranian dogs, and I'm supposed to give you a puppy."

My parents were shocked. No one had told this pastor that's what my sister had prayed for.

"That's Kirsten's dog!" my mom said in amazement to my dad. "We can't deny her faith has brought this."

So they brought the tiny puppy home to my sister, who cried and praised God.

When did Kirsten receive the dog? *When she prayed.* How do I know that? Jesus said, "*Therefore I say to you, whatever things you ask when you pray, believe that you receive them, and you will have them*" (Mark 11:24, NKJV). Another translation puts it like this: "*This is the reason I urge you to boldly believe for whatever you ask for in prayer—be convinced that you **have received** it and **it will** be yours*" (TPT).

Notice there are two grammatical verb tenses in that verse. He said to believe that when you pray, you HAVE received it, and then it WILL be yours. So when do you have it? When you pray. No matter when it actually shows up, your faith says you have received it when you pray.

Kirsten saw the picture of what she wanted, believed that she re-

THE 30-DAY HEALING DARE

ceived it when she prayed the prayer of faith, and then God worked on her behalf to orchestrate the events leading up to her holding that puppy in her arms. She believed she received when she prayed, no matter who tried to talk her off of it!

Kirsten followed these simple steps to receiving from God, as shown time and time again in the Bible:

1. *We believe in our hearts.* — This means we use the Word of God to become fully persuaded of God's will and promises concerning that situation. Faith comes by speaking and learning the Word of God. Our faith releases all fear and trusts our Father explicitly.

2. *We confess with our mouths.* — We speak the prayer of agreement, which is how we receive what we need. When we pray, our faith says, "Yes! It's done! I know I have whatever I asked in faith, because Mark 11:24 says so!" That's the moment we receive, not the moment the actual item shows up or the moment the circumstances change. Faith says it's done when we pray. Words of faith are magnets that bring a harvest!

3. *It shall be done for us.* — We stand on the promises of God and thank Him that it's ALREADY done. Past tense. How can we be so sure? Because God promised it, not us. It was done, so it is done. I *was* healed on the cross, so I *am* healed now.

Faith Says "Yes" to God's Gifts

In Mark 11:24, Jesus said we can have what we ask for in prayer if we don't doubt. You might think, "Now, Amy, did Jesus really mean that we will have whatever we ask for in prayer?" Unless we want to complicate things, I tend to take Jesus at face value when He says something. The apostle John echoes Jesus's sentiments in 1 John 5:14-15,

> *This is the confidence we have in approaching God: that if we ask anything according to his will, he hears us. And if we know that he hears us—whatever we ask—we know that we have what we asked of him.*

As long as it's not something that is rooted in sin (outside of His righteousness) or that violates another person's free will, we can receive it. That's a pretty bold statement, but that's what faith sounds like! It sounds bold. Hebrews 11:1 (TPT) talks about the power of bold faith. It says:

> *Now faith brings our hopes into reality and becomes the foundation needed to acquire the things we long for. It is all the evidence required to prove what is still unseen.*

Our faith gives substance to our prayers. It makes the thing we are receiving from God tangible even before we see it with our eyes. We must receive healing through faith, even while we still feel pain or are experiencing the effects of sickness. Faith reaches out and takes the extended gift of health from God's hands into our hands, even though maybe we haven't unwrapped it yet. Faith says "Yes!" to God's promises.

Kirsten knew that the dog would be hers, and once she prayed, she simply had to be patient. Promises require patience, but what we have prayed for will come if we don't let go of our picture of faith. Hebrews 6:12 says, "*We do not want you to become lazy, but to imitate those who **through faith and patience** inherit what has been promised.*"

You already know what patience is, but maybe you still have questions about faith. Let's review for a moment, because we are going to move into more about the prayer of FAITH, but it requires that we first HAVE faith.

Remember, faith in God's Word connects us to His promises. It's what allows Him to act on our behalves. To approach God and receive something from Him, we know that faith is the key. Faith is total belief in something. Basically, our faith will produce the outcome of whatever we come into agreement with. **What we believe will be.** Even fear is a form of faith, just faith in the wrong thing. We use the word *fear* to reference a belief that something bad or evil is going to happen. Fear is a belief that simply agrees with the earth curse effect rather than the supernatural way of escape that Jesus provided. The human heart was made to come into agreement with something, and that something will produce a harvest—either good or bad. That is how faith works. There is only faith, only belief. The question is WHAT do we believe?

Hebrews 11:6 (NLT) says,

> *And it is impossible to please God without faith. Anyone who wants to come to him must believe that God exists and that he rewards those who sincerely seek him.*

One morning, as I got close to the end of my 30-day Healing Dare, just like you are right now, it finally hit me. **I. WAS. HEALED**. I believed it. I was fully convinced that healing was mine and I had it in my hand. All I had to do was unwrap the gift Father God gave me! I was so filled with joy, I started crying and laughing and praising

God, jumping up and down in my little prayer closet! Why? Because my spirit knew I already had it. **Faith saw the after picture while I was still living in the before.**

That joy was indescribable! I honestly celebrated more on that day than when the actual healing showed up, because on that day, it was done. So what does faith feel like? Faith is not an emotion, but it does often feel like joy. Why? Because if you KNEW you had what you were praying for, wouldn't you celebrate? If you were instantly healed in this moment of reading, would you feel joy? Faith says, "You are healed NOW."

Now I still had one more step to take in order to receive, and this is where a lot of Christians miss it. I still needed to pray the prayer of faith and actually open the gift that God had already given me. **The Word said it was mine. My faith said, "Yes, it's mine." So those two things were in agreement. But I still needed to open the gift.**

The "Sickle Principle"

How do we open the gifts God has already said are ours?

In the amazing teaching series, "Your Financial Revolution," my dad talks about something he calls "The Sickle Principle." (Side note: Don't walk, RUN to GaryKeesee.com and download that audio teaching TODAY if you haven't heard it yet. It's simple, mind-blowing, and powerful!) He calls it that because this principle is taken from the parable of the sower in Mark 4. In this parable, Jesus is illustrating how faith grows and produces a crop, how something intangible turns into something that is tangible. He uses the illustration of planting and harvesting. Faith, just like a seed buried underground, grows a crop. When the crop is ready, it must be harvested. How? By putting in the *sickle*—or *harvesting tool*. Here's that parable:

> He also said, "This is what the kingdom of God is like. A man scatters seed on the ground. Night and day, whether he sleeps or gets up, the seed sprouts and grows, though he does not know how. All by itself the soil produces grain—first the stalk, then the head, then the full kernel in the head. As soon as the grain is ripe, **<u>he puts the sickle to it</u>**, because the harvest has come."
>
> —Mark 4:26-29

So, in order to receive a "harvest," according to Jesus's illustration, this is the process of growing faith, which then becomes the way we receive all of the promises of God:

1. Plant the seed of the Word in our hearts.
2. Watch as the seed grows, first as a little stalk then something with fruit on it.
3. Harvest the seed by putting the sickle in. (Let's talk about how to do this.)

Let's equate this parable to what you have been doing for the past 25 days within this 30-day Healing Dare. Through your Daily Faith Boosters and these devotions, you have been planting, watering, and tending your heart, growing a crop of faith in expectation of your harvest of healing. When you plant the Word in your heart and focus on the picture of what you need (healing), it starts to grow that picture inside of you. It happens all by itself, just like a seed planted in the ground grows. You start to feel bigger on the inside. You start to feel hopeful and then joyful.

Pretty soon, your heart can see the promise clearly. Doubts get quieter and boldness grows. You not only know that it's possible, but also you know that it's imminent. It's happening! You know that Jesus already gave you the gift, and now you just need to unwrap it.

This process is shown to us in the natural world every year by farmers. A corn farmer plants his seeds in good soil, diligently waters them, keeps the pests away, and watches for signs that his crop is mature, ready to harvest. On the day he sees that the crop in his field matches the picture on the seed packet, with a full stalk and ripe ears of corn, he gets out his harvesting tools (as my dad says in his "Your Financial Revolution" teaching). He fills up his combine with gas and pulls it out of the barn. He "puts the sickle in," to put it in Jesus's term.

A sickle was a tool that was used in Jesus's day to cut down the grain and bring it in from the fields. It was a sharp blade that would chop through the stalks so that people could pick them up and take them home. In the same way, once our faith has grown to the point of seeing the harvest in our hearts, it's time to break out our harvesting tool, put the sickle in, chop down that fruit, and take it home in the natural realm.

BUT IT IS IMPORTANT TO WAIT UNTIL OUR FAITH HAS GROWN TO MATURITY. Otherwise, we can't very well pray the "prayer of FAITH." It will be more of a "prayer of maybe." Haha!

On that day during my 30-day Healing Dare when I had that immense joy wash over me, I knew that I *knew* that I *knew* I was ready to receive. My faith saw me healed. My faith saw the victory! It shouted inside of me, "It's harvest time!" It was then time to "put the sickle in" and carry home my harvest.

How do we do that? What is our harvest tool once faith has grown to maturity? Our harvest tool is our words. Our words are the powerful combine that brings home the harvest. We must speak. We must add our "So be it" to God's "I will." (Affirm the New Covenant!) And we can know that we have what we ask, just like Jesus said. We can be confident when we ask.

> *This is the [remarkable degree of] confidence which we [as believers are entitled to] have before Him: that if we ask anything according to His will, [that is, consistent with His plan and purpose] He hears us. And if we know [for a fact, as indeed we do] that He hears and listens to us in whatever we ask, we [also] know [with settled and absolute knowledge] that we have [granted to us] the requests which we have asked from Him.*
> —1 John 5:14-15 (AMP)

The Prayer of Faith

The prayer of faith is also called "the prayer of agreement" because we are coming into agreement with God's Word when we pray in faith. It is talked about several times in the New Testament, and it's a powerful thing! The prayer of agreement also references this exchange of covenant being witnessed by someone else who is also in faith—a witness. In a church service or in a room filled with Jesus followers, there is an atmosphere of faith. There is a corporate anointing that flows. When two or more come together, it multiplies the power!

Jesus said:

> *"Again, truly I tell you that if two of you on earth agree about anything they ask for, it will be done for them by my Father in heaven. For where two or three gather in my name, there am I with them."*

—Matthew 18:19-20

I think this is why the following instruction was given to the early church, for when someone needed healing:

> *Is anyone among you sick? Let them call the elders of the church to pray over them and anoint them with oil in the name of the Lord. And the prayer offered in faith will make the sick person well; the Lord will raise them up. If they have sinned, they will be forgiven. Therefore confess your sins to each other and pray for each other so that you may be healed. The prayer of a righteous person is powerful and effective.*

—James 5:14-16

Who can come into agreement with you? Really, it can be anyone else who is also in faith with you. Obviously, they must also believe in our covenant of healing. But I believe the main reason the early church was given this instruction to go to the leaders of the church for prayer is that it helps our faith when we receive prayer from someone in authority over us. My husband, who is the priest of our house, brings the presence of God into the room when he prays over me. I feel it so strongly! Why? Because I honor him as my authority in our home. When the two of us, who are already in the covenant of marriage, come into agreement with God's covenant for us, THERE IS POWER!

You can receive prayer from a leader at church or a friend you look up to—as long as they *believe* in God's covenant with you concerning healing.

Let me just say that it's not like we can't receive healing without someone else's agreement, but it DOES give us a "touch point," a moment that we can remember as the moment we released our faith and received our healing. It marks the spot where we added our "Amen" to God's "I will." It marks the moment we put in the harvest tool. Healing is a legal right, so it makes sense that we should have witnesses, much like a legal contract requires witnesses. This prayer of agreement becomes a moment of remembrance if the devil tries to tell you, "You're still sick" or "It didn't really work." You can tell him, "No, no, no, devil; that's not right. On September 28 at 1:45 p.m., the elders of the church anointed me with oil, and I said the 'So be it' to God's 'I will.'"

Now, if you don't have anyone who can agree with you, know that the Holy Spirit is with you, and He can add His "Yes!" to your prayer of faith. As Jesse Duplantis said, "The Holy Spirit can be your 'two' for the 'where two or more are gathered.'" Awesome!

Often, Jason and I write out our petition to the Lord and sign our names at the bottom with the date, imagining that Jesus also signs His name at the bottom. He signed the New Covenant with the blood that He shed on the cross for our total healing! This idea of writing out our petition comes from this Scripture:

> *Do not be anxious about anything, but in every situation, **by***

**prayer and petition, with thanksgiving**, present your requests to God.

—Philippians 4:6

We can present our request as a petition to God, with a grateful heart, and then we don't have to worry about it. It's done. We can rest in confidence. We can trust.

Something else you'll notice in the passage from James 5 is the mention of "anointing them with oil." Why? The oil mentioned in the verse is a symbol and reminder that we are sealed with the Holy Spirit and that His healing anointing is flowing over us as we pray. It creates a "point of contact" for our faith, kind of like touching an electric socket. Power is going to flow through our bodies! Also, oil represents the anointing of the Holy Spirit. It is derived from shepherds who used to anoint their sheep with oil to ward off pests and lice. It protects. Likewise, the healing anointing flows over our bodies and protects us from disease. Oil used with laying on of hands is an outward sign of an inward exchange.

Words of Faith

James 4:2 says that the reason we don't have is because we don't ask. We haven't put in the sickle—we haven't activated our harvesting tool. Now the word "ask" or "prayer" doesn't mean "beg" and "whine." We don't beg God for what He has already given us.

Words of begging don't change things. Words of faith change things.

Jesus said in Matthew 6:7-8:

> *"And when you pray, do not keep on babbling like pagans, for they think they will be heard because of their many words. Do not be like them, for your Father knows what you need before you ask him."*

In other words, stop going on and on about what you need, begging for something God has already provided for.

Jesus said to pray like this, *"Give us today our daily bread"* (Matthew 6:11). That sounds rather commanding and confident, doesn't it? By the way, Jesus called healing the children's bread in Mark 7:27. In other words, everything we need to sustain us daily, including provision and health, is provided for us. Pass the biscuits!

<u>Begging for something implies that you don't yet have it.</u> It implies that you are still trying to convince God to do something when He has already done it! You are simply to receive it.

Even the way people use this phrase, "I'm believing for healing" can imply that they don't fully believe they *already* have it.

Instead, I've started saying, "I've received healing." Once I've put in my harvest tool—prayer of faith—then I need to stop speaking like it's something in the future. It is indeed something I have already received by faith.

 **READ**

Look up Hebrews 6:11-19, meditate on them, and focus on the "faith and patience" part. Then read and put your own name into the following Scripture:

Ask, _____ and it will be given to you _____;
seek, _____ and you will find, _____; knock,
_____ and it will be opened to you, _____. For
everyone who asks receives, and he who seeks finds, and to him
who knocks it will be opened.

—Matthew 7:7-8

 ## DETOX:

Have you been begging God for something that's already been given to you? Take a minute to repent of those words of unbelief, and know that Father God is so gracious and is never angry with us. He DELIGHTS in blessing our lives with good things, and He is so excited about your journey to health.

 ## SELF-REFLECTION:

Okay, if you have hit that moment of becoming fully persuaded for your healing, I want you to pray your Prayer of Agreement either with someone who you know believes it is yours or just between you and the Holy Spirit. Write any notes here as you pray about when and where and with whom to pray.

TODAY'S TAKEAWAY:

My faith calls it done whenever I pray the prayer of faith.

PRAYER

*Lord Jesus, help me to be a diligent farmer,
and help me to know when my heart is fully in
agreement with Your Word so that I can pray
the prayer of faith.*

THE PRAYER OF FAITH

IT IS FINISHED

L et's remind ourselves what faith looks like:

As Jesus was on his way, the crowds almost crushed him. And a woman was there who had been subject to bleeding for twelve years, but no one could heal her. She came up behind him and touched the edge of his cloak, and immediately her bleeding stopped. "Who touched me?" Jesus asked. When they all denied it, Peter said, "Master, the people are crowding and pressing against you." But Jesus said, "Someone touched me; <u>I know that power has gone out from me</u>." Then the woman, seeing that she could not go unnoticed, came trembling and fell at his feet. In the presence of all the people, she told why she had touched him and how she had been instantly healed. Then he said to her, "<u>Daughter, your faith has healed you. Go in peace</u>."

—Luke 8:42-48

So Jesus felt power leave Him and flow to her.

Did Jesus know she was there before that moment? No.

Did He have to arbitrarily decide to heal her? No.

By virtue of <u>who He was and who she was</u> (a daughter), her faith (agreement) received her healing. Her faith grabbed hold of His healing power!

Faith always takes action!

Someone might ask, "Did she pray a prayer of agreement when she received her healing?" Well, what is the prayer of agreement? It is agreeing and receiving God's power, as made available through His will. The Gospel of Mark gives us another detail to this story:

> When she heard about Jesus' healing power, she pushed through the crowd and came up from behind him and touched his prayer shawl. _For she kept saying to herself, "If only I could touch his clothes, I know I will be healed."_ As soon as her hand touched him, her bleeding immediately stopped! She knew it, for she could feel her body instantly being healed of her disease!...Then Jesus said to her, "Daughter, _because you dared to believe, your faith has healed you._ Go with peace in your heart, and be free from your suffering!"
>
> —Mark 5:27-29, 34 (TPT)

So she heard the word about Jesus, believed it was true, and <u>said</u> (words spoken in agreement with God's will) that if she could just touch His clothes (a point of contact), she would be healed (the end result that her faith saw).

The prayer of faith is simply connecting with God and receiving from Him. And that's what she did when she confidently pushed her way through the crowd. She dared to believe.

Friend, once you have prayed that prayer of agreement in faith, you can be confident it is finished!

When Jesus was hanging on the cross—unrecognizable due to the beating He had received, mocked by a sign hanging over His head that read "King of the Jews"—with the last bit of breath left in Him, He said, "_It is finished_" (John 19:30).

The Greek term Jesus used is *tetelestai*, and it's a financial accounting term meaning "paid in full." He paid the debt we owed! He paid for our healing! He paid for our peace! He paid for our provision! We are now free from the curse! He settled the score!

Imagine that you are a murderer sitting in solitary confinement, waiting to be executed. There is no hope of appeal or release. The prosecutor won. But at the last minute, as you are about to be taken to the execution room, a person dressed in guard's clothing slips into your cell. He looks like he could be your twin! But then he says something that makes you hold your breath. He tells you that you can go free.

"What?!" you gasp. "I'm about to be executed. I murdered someone! If I try to leave, they will just catch me."

"Not if I am executed in your place," he says.

Before you can think, he hands you a guard's uniform and his ID, free of any criminal record. He hands you the keys to his car, gives you some last minute instructions on how to get out, and then tells you to leave.

You do as you're told, forever leaving behind your old name and taking on his identity. You slip out the door as a free man. You read later in the news that he had done it. He had been executed in your place. He gave you his life and identity and took your guilt and death sentence.

That's what Jesus did for us. He came to Earth, looking just like we do when we're born, disguised as a frail baby in a manger.

He grew into a man, taught about the Kingdom of God, and gained plenty of rejection and persecution along the way. *But it was all part of the plan.*

He allowed Himself to be taken into custody, tried, and condemned. *But it was all part of the plan.*

He was tortured and took excruciating pain in His body. *But it was all part of the plan.*

He was nailed to a cross, humiliated in front of all of Jerusalem, abandoned and betrayed by those closest to Him. *But it was all part of the plan.*

He was laid in a tomb in the earth He had created. For three days, His disciples mourned His death while He descended to hell to reclaim from the devil what was stolen from the first human, Adam. *It was all part of the plan.*

On the third day, He triumphed, the breath returning into His body, now perfectly whole and restored. He proved to His disciples that it was indeed Him, the crucified Jesus. And that was the day Satan realized something...

It had all been part of God's plan!

Jesus did it all so He could take back the keys of the Kingdom, which He then handed to us (Matthew 16:19). But not only did He pay for our forgiveness, He also paid for ALL things to be restored like it was in the Garden of Eden. That included your health.

Our healing was finished. And the day we add our "So be it" through the prayer of agreement, we can count it done!

My sister-in-law Alecia has a habit of taking communion daily to remind herself of the New Covenant that we talked about before, the one Jesus gave us with His resurrection. She started doing that during a health crisis a few years back.

It started pretty innocently with just a small lump in her abdomen, so she went to her doctor. She was referred to a specialist, who basically freaked out and said she had a very rare form of cancer. The doctor's words were that she could die within a few months or less! He referred her to The James Cancer Hospital. She really had to fight the words of that doctor. She knew this was just a mirage of the enemy, and we all started praying. Alecia started listening to healing messages 24/7 and started taking communion every day.

After scans and a biopsy at The James, the doctor had good news. No, she did not have a rare form of cancer, and no, she was not dying. She did have a very slow growing form of cancer in the tumor, and he warned it was going to get larger. The tumor was almost the size of a baseball, it stuck out of her right abdomen wall, and it caused her pain. The only way to stop it from growing was to remove it, he said. But it was embedded in her abdominal muscle, and to remove it would mean removing some of that, which could cause lasting issues. So there was some good news mixed with bad news.

On top of all this news, Alecia had suffered a miscarriage just before the discovery of the tumor. The doctor said it was probably due to the tumor's strain on her body. Alecia and my brother Tim were still praying for a third child, but the doctor warned her not to get pregnant because the tumor could grow exponentially quicker with more blood flow and the hormones from pregnancy.

Alecia started targeting that tumor with the Word of God, building her faith.

"Fear of sickness and dying has always been a thing in my family," she said. "I had to break that generational curse."

She admitted that it took a while to overcome those roots of fear. But as she reminded herself of the Word, and took communion daily, she got stronger and more confident on the inside. She made a choice to ignore her emotions and the fearful thoughts that tried to come. She and Tim prayed the prayer of agreement, and then they counted it as done. She believed she was healed. And despite the fact that the tumor was still there, Tim and Alecia felt to trust God for a third child as if the tumor was already gone.

When they found out that she was pregnant, they were overjoyed! Alecia spoke the Word over her body and constantly rejected thoughts that something was going to go wrong. She had a great pregnancy with no complications. Nine months later, baby Aurora Noelle was born perfectly healthy, whole, and strong. It was a wonderful delivery, and Alecia felt great.

It was during postpartum recovery as her stomach went down that she realized something. The tumor was gone!

It had completely disappeared. Defying medical reason, the tumor had not grown during her pregnancy, because God had removed it!

A Place of Remembrance

When Jesus rose from the grave, He broke the power of death's hold off of us. He crushed the serpent's head (Genesis 3:15) and righted the wrongs that came with the curse.

Alecia received that victory in her spirit, and she stood on God's promises. Once she and Tim prayed the prayer of faith, they went about life as if she was already healed, even though the evidence said otherwise. She knew there was a higher Word than any doctor's word. Jesus, the Great Physician, had her back.

When we say, "Amen," God enables us to stand firm on His "Yes." And He doesn't change His mind:

> *But as surely as God is faithful, our message to you is not "Yes" and "No." For the Son of God, Jesus Christ, who was preached among you by us—by me and Silas and Timothy—was not "Yes" and "No," but in him it has always been "Yes." For no matter how many promises God has made, they are "Yes" in Christ. And so through him the "Amen" is spoken by us to the glory of God. Now it is God who makes both us and you stand firm in Christ. He anointed us.*
>
> —2 Corinthians 1:18-21

Once you have prayed the prayer of agreement with God's Word, it's time to stand and put yourself in a place of remembrance just as Alecia did when she took daily communion. She was remembering the body and blood of Jesus given for her healing.

Even though that day when I had the elders lay hands on me and pray I did not see an immediate change, I knew that I could stand on God's promise as though it was done. I would live and not die, because of the life given to me by Jesus. I knew that God said, "... *Take hold of my words with all your heart; keep my commands, and you will live*" (Proverbs 4:4). I acted like it was done.

Two weeks later, it showed up in the natural. But I already knew that was going to happen. I had received Jesus's, "It is finished."

 **READ**

Luke 22:17-20 and 1 Corinthians 11:24-30

 SELF-REFLECTION:
Spend some time in worship and reverence for all God has done for you through the New Covenant, giving you His promises of "I will." Then take communion, and use your Scripture reading above as your guide.

 TODAY'S TAKEAWAY:
I will celebrate the victory and take action on it, knowing that without a doubt, Jesus broke the power of sickness off of my life.

TESTIMONY:

"Amy, I have wonderful news about my friend who was healed... Your book revived her belief just days before her pancreas was to be removed. God healed her! No more pancreatic cancer! She has before and after pictures from the doctors. Praise God!"

—Jim

PRAYER

Thank You for Your body that was broken for mine, that by Your stripes I am healed. I worship You and praise Your name! You are so good to me, Jesus! I love you!

THE PRAYER OF FAITH

GREATER THAN THE NATURAL REALM

DAY 27

We have an amazing Father God who has made decrees about our lives that will never be too impossible and will never not be true. What He says goes. When He said, "Let there be light," *poof!* Light was there. He said, *"By myself I have sworn, my mouth has uttered in all integrity a word that will not be revoked"* (Isaiah 45:23a).

What God says stands for all eternity. His decrees are flawless and forever. What He said about you and your life will never pass away. Why? Because God is outside of time and the natural realm's limitations!

> *And He Himself existed and is before all things, and in Him all things hold together. [His is the controlling, cohesive force of the universe.]*
>
> —Colossians 1:17 (AMP)

God was never created, because He always was. He is outside of time. Jesus said in Revelation 22:13, *"I am the Alpha and the Omega, the First and the Last, the Beginning and the End."* This is a concept that kind of blows our human logic, because we cannot fathom it. We have always lived in a world marked by time, seasons, start dates, and end dates. But what that means is God is not confined by any of those frameworks, because He created them! He is Lord over time because He created time to serve His work.

Do you know what this means in relation to your healing?

GOD HAS MADE A WAY FOR YOUR HEALING TO MANIFEST QUICKER THAN NATURAL TIME ALLOWS.

314

He is able to instantly do what should take weeks, months, or years. For instance, did you know your spine renews 10% of its cells per year? But one of our elders, Pastor Ron, had an instant healing of several herniated disks. It happened within *one minute.*

How? God sped up the renewal rate.

The spirit realm is so much faster than the earthly realm! That's how so many people in the Bible recovered *instantly.* That's how Adam, after being in that horrific car accident, astounded doctors with a much shorter recovery period than they could predict.

God sees the beginning from the end before it ever happens, and He can quicken the healing process in your mortal body.

My favorite healing Scripture, Romans 8:11 (KJV), says that the Spirit of Him that raised Christ from the dead will QUICKEN your mortal body! He can fast-track the recovery process in your cells, bones, and organs. He can reverse damage. He can rewind your body to how it was before it got sick. He can renew, restore, and regenerate parts that are diseased.

The resurrected Jesus walked through walls, caught up to groups of people on the road, and appeared out of nowhere to people like Paul on the road to Damascus. How? Because He is not bound by the limitations of Earth.

When we walk in the Spirit, we can supersede natural laws and tap into greater spiritual laws.

The things we can see with our natural eyes and hear with our natural ears are very limited.

We cannot see cells, molecules, atoms, radio waves, or sound waves with our eyes. We can't see the wind or the law of lift or the many galaxies outside of our solar system. But that doesn't make any of those things less real.

We can't hear many of the high and low frequency sounds whirring through the air. But they are there.

We can't (usually) see angels, but they are there. (One time, a lady at one of our women's conferences took a photo, and it captured the perfect, glowing silhouette of an angel. The camera shutter speed captured what our human eye was too slow to see.)

The power of our Infinite Creator is unimaginable! He created worlds without end and many, many more things we have yet to discover. Science is only trying to catch up to His creative genius.

Jesus showed us over and over again that God's power is greater than natural laws. He did some pretty astonishing miracles! Think about the following miracles in relation to your own healing, however impossible it might feel:

> *News about him spread all over Syria, and people brought to him all who were ill with various diseases, those suffering severe pain, the demon-possessed, those having seizures, and the paralyzed; and he healed them.*
>
> —Matthew 4:24

A large crowd followed him, and he healed all who were ill.

—Matthew 12:15b

Great crowds came to him, bringing the lame, the blind, the crippled, the mute and many others, and laid them at his feet; and he healed them.

—Matthew 15:30

Large crowds followed him, and he healed them there.

—Matthew 19:2

As a result, people brought the sick into the streets and laid them on beds and mats so that at least Peter's shadow might fall on some of them as he passed by. Crowds gathered also from the towns around Jerusalem, bringing their sick and those tormented by impure spirits, and all of them were healed.

—Acts 5:15-16

Very truly I tell you, whoever believes in me will do the works I have been doing, and they will do even greater things than these, because I am going to the Father.

—John 14:12

Jesus rebuked the demon, and it came out of the boy, and he was healed at that moment.

—Matthew 17:18

Naturally thinking, our human minds try to limit what is possible only to what we can understand. And yet, we are children of Jehovah, the "I AM," the Omniscient and Omnipresent God. We can trust that His *unlimited* power is at work even when we cannot see it. Romans 4:17b says that He is, *"the God who gives life to the dead and calls into being things that were not."*

The Moment of Receiving

We've been talking about the prayer of faith for the past few days. But we haven't actually prayed that prayer yet. First, you need to know you are in faith. How do you know? Here's a clue: What do you see when you close your eyes? If you can see yourself healthy and whole, fully restored, and you are convinced that it is yours according to God's Word, then your heart is ready to receive. It is picturing the results of God's promises, and that's FAITH! If that is you, following is an example of a petition for you to agree with before the Lord. I also encourage you to do as James 5 says (if possible) and receive the prayer of agreement from someone who is also is in faith for your healing. That becomes your moment of receiving!

If when you close your eyes you still see yourself battling a sickness, then you are not in faith yet. And, that is okay! It's important to know that and to be honest with yourself. If that is you, there is no shame in that. You just need more time to take these steps. You should continue on your healing challenge, do the Daily Faith Boosters, and perhaps reread this devotional. The Word will grow faith in your heart, but for some it takes more time. Perhaps you have been taught against this healing stuff and have some religious mindsets to overcome (like the Pharisees did). Maybe you have been sick for so long that you can't picture what it would be like to get well. Just keep being a diligent farmer, guarding your heart, planting the Word, and standing boldly in your identity. When you feel the joy and assurance that faith brings, let's pray.

The Prayer of Agreement: Are you ready to receive? As I write this, the healing anointing is so strong, I am weeping and shaking. I know this is YOUR moment for the power of God to touch you. When you pray this prayer of faith (and don't do it yet if you aren't quite ready), fill this in as a point of remembrance. You can stand on this moment in the days to come!

> *Jesus, I believe Your Word is true for me, and my heart is fully convinced that it's Your will for me to walk in total health and healing.*
>
> *I, _____*
> *receive from You the following: _____*
> *_____*
> *_____*
> *according to Your healing promise found in:_____*
> *_____*
> *_____*
> *that says: _____*
> *_____*
> *_____*
> *_____*
> *_____*
> *On this day (date):_____ at*
> *(time):_____.*

I pray the prayer of agreement, surrounded by these witnesses:

_____
_____
_____

I was healed! I receive it now, and I thank you for it, Jesus! So be it! Amen!

Wow; praise God! I feel so strongly that many people are receiving incredible healing power flowing through their bodies right now! That includes you, in the name of Jesus!

Romans 1:20 and Isaiah 40:31

SELF-REFLECTION:

Take the limitations off of your mind and dream. Go outside and look at the stars in the sky filled with billions of galaxies so vast science cannot count or see them all. Reflect on the vast power of God, then apply that to your current situation. Use your faith imagination to describe what happens when the power of God comes into contact with a difficult situation in your life.

TODAY'S TAKEAWAY:

I will not limit what God can do or what I can do with Him. I will not filter my circumstances through my natural mind, but I will keep my focus on the mighty God who is able to call dead things back to life again.

 # PRAYER

Jesus, thank You that I have received my healing, and I keep my mind in a place of remembrance. I think about all You have created and the vastness of Your plan. You are amazing! I thank You that I will see Your work in my life as I come into agreement with Your Word. I step into life by the Spirit and take off the limitations in my mind. You are quickening my body, restoring it to the way You intended for it to work.

Day
28

PRAISE HIM FOR VICTORY

ACT LIKE YOU HAVE IT

DAY 28

We are here at our final key for healing! Each of these literally transformed my life and body as God taught them to me during my own 30-day Healing Dare. Do you have the other ones memorized? Let's review them and put in our final key principle:

1. Reclaim your identity. (Know who you are in Christ.)

2. Repaint your picture. (Faith is fully persuaded of God's promises.)

3. Stand in your authority. (Enforce the victory.)

4. Pray the prayer of faith. (It's done when you pray!)

5. Praise Him for the victory! (NEW one! What to do after you've prayed....)

Once we have prayed the prayer of agreement, in faith, and we know it is finished, what do we do then? What if we don't see an immediate manifestation of healing? What if things feel the same?

I faced those same questions after I received prayer. I walked away from the altar after receiving prayer feeling the same way as when I walked in.

First of all, I did not despair when I walked away from the altar feeling and looking exactly the same.

Instead, I reminded myself that I was living in the finished work of the Cross. If I already had it, I should start acting like it! It was finished. Healed was part of my identity as God's child. My faith saw the after when I was still living in the before. So I wrote the date and time down in my Bible as the date and time that I was healed. Even though I didn't feel like anything changed.

Every day, I continued to read my Scriptures out loud over my body several times, reminding myself of His Word. I spoke my Confession of Faith, but I made sure to never *ask* God to heal me. Why? Because I had already received it!

Instead of continually asking God to heal me, I praised Him and thanked Him as if I could see it in my body already. I planned on feeling great again. I planned on wearing well-fitting clothing instead of baggy shirts. I planned on having children. I planned on fulfilling my life's calling. I planned on walking in healing!

So once we have received the gift, we don't check our bodies every five seconds to "see if it worked." That is a good indication that we weren't actually in faith to begin with, right? We just simply reinforce the fact that it was done by praising and thanking God, acting as if we are healed. Maybe it means doing things that we couldn't do before. That might sound counterintuitive if we haven't felt anything change, but often, things change IN THE ACT of moving forward by faith.

In John 5, Jesus told a man who was paralyzed, "Take up your bed and walk." What if the paralyzed man had said, "But, Jesus, did you forget I'm paralyzed"? Instead, the man moved in obedience. And as he went to move, he realized he was indeed healed!

Luke 17:13-14 (TPT) talk about men who were also healed on their way, AFTER talking to Jesus:

> *They shouted to him, "Mighty Lord, our wonderful Master! Won't you have mercy on us and heal us?" When Jesus stopped to look at them, he spoke these words: "Go to be examined by the Jewish priests." They set off, and they were healed while walking along the way.*

Sometimes, when the manifestation of healing doesn't show up instantly, it requires us to simply keep moving forward in faith. We need to continue to take steps toward our pain-free destiny. Our faith says it is already done, so there is no more asking God, begging God, wishing for it, or hoping for it. There is only knowing it's done, and praising God, and thanking Him for completing the work He started. That reminds me of something Yoda from the Star Wars movie trilogy said, "Do or don't do. There is no try." Haha! There is no "trying to believe." We either believe or don't believe. We either have faith or we don't have faith. And if we find it's the latter, that we are being blown around by winds of unbelief, it's time to plant some more faith seed in our hearts.

The Lord Who Heals

One of the names that God calls Himself is Jehovah Rapha, which means "the Lord who heals." Rapha means "to heal," "to make whole," "to properly mend by stitching," and "to repair."[15] This name appears in Exodus 15:26:

---

[15] https://www.crosswalk.com/faith/bible-study/why-do-we-call-on-god-as-jehovah-ra-pha-for-healing.html

He said, "If you listen carefully to the Lord your God and do what is right in his eyes, if you pay attention to his commands and keep all his decrees, I will not bring on you any of the diseases I brought on the Egyptians, for <u>I am the Lord, who heals you</u>."

This name appears in Jeremiah 30:17, Psalm 103:3, and Isaiah 30:26. Look them up! It was God's idea to call Himself that. He called Himself the Healer. It's part of His nature and His heart for all of us. He does not want anyone to suffer. We must continually remind ourselves that one of His attributes is "Healer." And if He, Himself is our Healer, we have the answer for any fear of death that comes knocking at our door.

Now inevitably, the devil is going to sneak around and try to call God names other than Healer. He might even try calling God by one of his own (the devil's) names—Liar. The enemy is going to question God's promises and His character, just like he did with Adam and Eve in the Garden. He might say that God lied and that His Word didn't work. That's when you turn it around on him and remind satan that he is the liar. God can't lie.

Yes, there will be days when you don't "feel" like you're in faith. Your emotions or the pain in your body might be yelling for attention. Bills need paid, stresses present themselves, and you can lose sight of the joy you had yesterday. If you aren't careful, you allow your mind to get bogged down with the pressures and the problems and the pursuits of living.

Jesus knows what that's like, because He, too, walked this earth as human. He helps us in our weakness, through the Holy Spirit, if we will simply put ourselves in a place of remembrance. When we call on the name Jehovah Rapha, we are reminding ourselves that He is our Healer!

How to Keep Your Mind Free from Discouragement

I have found that it is essential during this period between the "Amen" and "There it is" to keep your mind quiet and free from discouragement.

If you're thinking that's easier said than done, you're right. But it is vital. And there are keys to doing it. Let me share some of the things I did during the two weeks between praying the prayer of agreement and then actually waking up healed overnight:

LAUGH. Take time to laugh every day! Put on a comedy movie, read jokes out loud, have a tickle fight with your kids, find the positive every day, and ask God to continually remind you of the joy of your salvation. Joy renews your immune system, eliminates stress, and helps your body heal quicker. Take laughter like medicine!

> *A joyful, cheerful heart brings healing to both body and soul. But the one whose heart is crushed struggles with sickness and depression.*
>
> —Proverbs 17:22 (TPT)

> *Restore to me the joy of your salvation and grant me a willing spirit, to sustain me.*
>
> —Psalm 51:12

> *Finally, brothers and sisters, whatever is true, whatever is noble,*

whatever is right, whatever is pure, whatever is lovely, whatever is admirable—if anything is excellent or praiseworthy—think about such things. Whatever you have learned or received or heard from me, or seen in me—put it into practice. And the God of peace will be with you.

—Philippians 4:8-9a

RELAX. Don't allow stress to overwhelm you. That "overwhelmed" feeling is often a symptom of our lack of time being overwhelmed by God's presence, in our quiet time. Stress is a symptom of misplaced trust. So keep that quiet time with God when you can just be. He will show you how to get everything done and how to navigate. Don't let the "winds and waves" of life get your eyes off of Jesus so that you start drowning, like Peter did in Matthew 14:30. It says, *"But when he saw the wind, he was afraid and, beginning to sink, cried out, 'Lord, save me!'"* He stopped looking at Jesus's strength. He stopped trusting Jesus's power.

Thankfully, if we ever start to sink into stress, we can just cry out, "Jesus save me," and He always does. Continually throw your anxious thoughts and cares off onto the Lord. Don't allow things to weigh heavy on you without taking them to God in prayer. In fact, stop yourself several times a day and ask, "Am I carrying weights I was never created to bear? I give them to You, God." Picture Him lifting a heavy backpack off of your back and putting it onto His back.

For some practical wisdom, try to allow downtime every day to do something you want to do, even if for just ten minutes. Let yourself enjoy a moment to reset. The world will keep moving forward; it doesn't revolve around you constantly striving. Tell yourself out loud, "Relax. Relax. Relax."

Come to me, all who labor and are heavy laden, and I will give you rest. Take My yoke upon you, and learn from Me, for I am gentle and lowly in heart, and you will find rest for your souls. For My yoke is easy, and My burden is light.
—Matthew 11:28-30 (NKJV)

From the end of the earth I will cry to You, when my heart is overwhelmed; lead me to the rock that is higher than I.
—Psalm 61:2 (NKJV)

When my spirit was overwhelmed within me, then you knew my path.
—Psalm 142:3 (NKJV)

TRUST. When you start to feel your heart becoming troubled, purposefully and intentionally say, "I trust in You, Lord." Like a baby resting in the arms of its mother, free from concern, we need to lay ourselves down in the arms of Jesus and let go of all those stupid little things that try to steal our joy.

Do not let your hearts be troubled. Trust in God; trust also in me.
—John 14:1

Commit your way to the Lord; trust in him, and he will act.
—Psalm 37:5 (ESV)

The steps of a man are established by the Lord, when he delights in his way.
—Psalm 37:23 (ESV)

Behold, God is my salvation; I will trust, and will not be afraid;

for the Lord God is my strength and my song, and he has become my salvation.

—Isaiah 12:2 (ESV)

REST. Allow the Holy Spirit to renew your strength. I wrote a song many years ago that was based on what God spoke directly to me during a time of struggle. He said to me, "Let Me be the Strong One. I am all that you need, so you don't have to be." Sometimes we put all this pressure on ourselves to be so strong for everyone else. But in the arms of Father God, we can just let Him be the strong one. He renews our strength. He carries us when we are too tired.

On a practical level, get good sleep! You can't abuse your body and expect it to just keep going forever without needing rest.

Have you not known? Have you not heard? The Lord is the ev-erlasting God, the Creator of the ends of the earth. He does not faint or grow weary; his understanding is unsearchable.

—Isaiah 40:28 (ESV)

But they who wait for the Lord shall renew their strength; they shall mount up with wings like eagles; they shall run and not be weary; they shall walk and not faint.

—Isaiah 40:31 (ESV)

There is no one holy like the Lord; there is no one besides you; there is no Rock like our God.

—1 Samuel 2:2

The Lord is my strength and my shield; my heart trusts in him, and he helps me. My heart leaps for joy, and with my song I will praise him.

—Psalm 28:7

Finally, be strong in the Lord and in his mighty power.
—Ephesians 6:10

STAY AT PEACE. God's peace will sustain you in a dry season. Remember, you are never alone. You are loved and more valuable to God than you'll ever be able to fathom. And He, Himself is your peace. That peace will guard your heart against fear.

Blessed are the peacemakers, for they shall be called sons of God.
—Matthew 5:9 (ESV)

Peace I leave with you; my peace I give to you. Not as the world gives do I give to you. Let not your hearts be troubled, neither let them be afraid.
—John 14:27 (ESV)

I have said these things to you, that in me you may have peace. In the world you will have tribulation. But take heart; I have overcome the world.
—John 16:33 (ESV)

On the evening of that day, the first day of the week, the doors being locked where the disciples were for fear of the Jews, Jesus came and stood among them and said to them, "Peace be with you."

—John 20:19 (ESV)

Do not be anxious about anything, but in everything by prayer and supplication with thanksgiving let your requests be made known to God. And the peace of God, which surpasses all understanding, will guard your hearts and your minds in Christ Jesus.

—Philippians 4:6-7 (ESV)

For the kingdom of God is not a matter of eating and drinking but of righteousness and peace and joy in the Holy Spirit. Whoever thus serves Christ is acceptable to God and approved by men. So then let us pursue what makes for peace and for mutual up building.

—Romans 14:17-19 (ESV)

WALK IN LOVE. Inevitably, whenever I am building my faith and receiving big things from God, the devil sends people problems to get me off course. Mean words, offenses, unforgiveness, betrayals, you name it will arise. But we cannot allow people to get us out of faith into the flesh.

Walk in love with those around you, and avoid division, arguments, and strife. Strife opens up the door to the devil, especially in marriage! Remind yourself when you're tempted to get angry or get even, "I'd rather be healed. I'd rather prosper."

Walk in love with yourself, too, remembering to be kind with your thoughts and words toward yourself.

Finally, brothers, rejoice. Aim for restoration, comfort one another, agree with one another, live in peace; and the God of love and peace will be with you.

—2 Corinthians 13:11 (ESV)

A new command I give you: Love one another. As I have loved you, so you must love one another. By this everyone will know that you are my disciples, if you love one another.

—John 13:34-35

And hope does not put us to shame, because God's love has been poured out into our hearts through the Holy Spirit, who has been given to us.

—Romans 5:5

A perverse person stirs up conflict, and a gossip separates close friends.

—Proverbs 16:28

PRAISE. There is nothing like putting on some good praise and worship music and marching around your house, singing and declaring your love for the King! It reminds your soul of who you serve. It reminds your flesh that it must bow to Jesus. It reminds your heart of the One who loves you more than life. And it reminds the devil that Jesus is King!

Praising God is a powerful weapon against the enemy. As we see in several stories in the Bible, praise can change atmospheres and shift destinies.

Around midnight Paul and Silas were praying and singing hymns to God, and the other prisoners were listening. Suddenly, there was a massive earthquake, and the prison was shaken to its foundations. All the doors immediately flew open, and the chains of every prisoner fell off!

—Acts 16:25-26 (NLT)

Praise God in his sanctuary; praise him in his mighty heavens!
Praise him for his acts of power; praise his surpassing greatness!

—Psalm 150:1b-2

When you hear the priests give one long blast on the rams' horns,
have all the people shout as loud as they can. Then the walls of
the town will collapse, and the people can charge straight into
the town.

—Joshua 6:5 (NLT)

SPEAK. We've already talked often about the power of speaking Scripture, but let me reiterate it again. Reading Scriptures out loud is like a drink of cold water on a hot day. The refreshing power of the promises of God can sustain us when all else feels dry.

It may not seem like a big deal, but let me tell you, reading the Word of God out loud is a GAME CHANGER. It is what changed my mindset and helped me truly believe for my physical healing, even in the face of pain and circumstances. It will keep your mind quiet and trusting in the Lord.

So in case you didn't already, go back and read ALL of the Scriptures in this chapter out loud over yourself.

When the thoughts start swirling and life is crazy, speak the Word! And whenever you are tempted to feel overwhelmed or discouraged about your health, remember this Scripture and make it personal to you: *"Jesus said, 'I will come and heal him'"* (Matthew 8:7, NLT).

 **READ**

Find your favorite Scripture from this day's reading and write it somewhere that you will see it every day. Put your name into it.

 # SELF-REFLECTION:

Do you commit to doing some of these things while you are "in the waiting"? What do you plan to implement? Make a plan.

 # TODAY'S TAKEAWAY:

I will not grow discouraged if I don't see or feel things change instantly. Instead, I will praise God for the victory as if it's already done, and I will not be moved.

PRAYER

Thank You, Father that my healing was finished, and now I praise and thank You for it. I celebrate with joy in my heart and a song on my lips. You are the sustainer of my life. I have but to watch and see You work. I have full confidence that I'm one day closer to seeing the natural manifestation of the spiritual reality I have already received.

PRAISE HIM FOR VICTORY

IN HIS
PRESENCE

There is a beautiful place where we can remain in peace, find our joy, resist fear, and receive confidence. It's in the *presence* of God.

I've been a worship leader since 2003, and I am extremely passionate about today's topic!

Do you know the one thing Jesus did that made everything else in His ministry possible?

He spent time with His Father daily.

It was there, in the cool of the Garden of Gethsemane or the Mount of Olives that He would go late into the night or very early in the morning. He pulled away to a quiet place. He rested in our Father's presence. THAT was where His authority and power stemmed from.

In the presence of Father God, Jesus was reminded of who He was and why He was here. The fellowship with the Father kept Him steady when the pressures of people, ministry, and the needs around Him became very heavy. Hebrews 4:15 (ESV) shows us that Jesus dealt with the same pressures we have:

> *For we do not have a high priest who is unable to sympathize with our weaknesses, but one who in every respect has been tempted as we are, yet without sin.*

Jesus was tempted by all the things we are tempted by today in some form or another. Yet, He chose to stay connected to Father God so that He could keep His eyes on His purpose. It was His life source, and it must be ours today. We must remain connected to Him.

Jesus put it this way:

> *I am the vine; you are the branches. If you remain in me and I in you, you will bear much fruit; <u>apart from me you can do nothing</u>. If you do not remain in me, you are like a branch that is thrown away and withers; such branches are picked up, thrown into the fire and burned. <u>If you remain in me and my words remain in you, ask whatever you wish, and it will be done for you</u>. This is to my Father's glory, that you bear much fruit, showing yourselves to be my disciples.*
>
> —John 15:5-8

When we remain in Father God's presence, in a close, intimate relationship with Him, it gives us the courage and confidence to stand in our authority. Our motivation for living becomes clear, to bring Him glory in everything we do, seen or unseen, big or small. Our priorities get in line so that we seek His Kingdom first, above all the other things that vie for our attention. Our hearts soften and stay sensitive to His leading so that we don't stray from the path. He revitalizes and strengthens us. He revives us when we don't think we can go on. He fills us with courage when we feel discouraged.

I can't overemphasize how important it is to bring Him along with you in your day, to talk with Him, ask Him questions, and let Him comfort you. We cannot receive power and authority without a relationship with Father God. Consider this your invitation: "*Then Jesus said, 'Let's go off by ourselves to a quiet place and rest awhile'*" (Mark 6:31a, NLT). Worshipping our Father and being with Him is essential for the battle. It's as important as breathing.

How to Fight Your Battles

When I was a little girl, we were at a friend's house when, all of a sudden, my dad started having intense pain. He was pretty sure it was a kidney stone because the pain was so terrible.

We all loaded into the car, and my mom told us, "We are going to worship and praise God for Dad's healing." So she turned up the worship music, and we all started praising God and thanking Him that the kidney stone was dissolving. We sang loudly and prayed all the way home. As soon as we got home, Dad got out of the passenger seat and said, "There's no more pain! As soon as we started praising, it went away!"

Later on in my life, as I've faced tough seasons, scary circumstances, or a threat of illness, it has been my instant reaction to start worshipping and praising God. I can't tell you how many times doing that one simple thing has resulted in breakthrough in my life.

I love the song "Surrounded (Fight My Battles)" by Elyssa Smith and UPPERROOM that says:

> *And I believe You've overcome,*
> *So I will lift my song of praise for all You've done.*
> *This is how I fight my battles! This is how I fight my battles!*
> *It may look like I'm surrounded, but I'm surrounded by You!*

That song reminds me of the story of King Jehoshaphat, one of Israel's kings in the Old Testament. He found himself faced with a massive invading army, and it looked totally impossible for victory to happen. When the king sought the Lord, God spoke to him and gave him a plan that seemed foolish. Here's the story as told in 2 Chronicles 20:

> *"**You will not have to fight this battle**. Take up your positions; stand firm and see the deliverance the Lord will give you, Judah and Jerusalem. Do not be afraid; do not be discouraged. Go out to face them tomorrow, and the Lord will be with you."*
>
> *Jehoshaphat bowed down with his face to the ground, and all the people of Judah and Jerusalem **fell down in worship before the Lord**. Then some Levites from the Kohathites and Korahites stood up and **praised the Lord, the God of Israel, with a very loud voice**.*
>
> *Early in the morning they left for the Desert of Tekoa. As they set out, Jehoshaphat stood and said, "Listen to me, Judah and people of Jerusalem! Have faith in the Lord your God and you will be upheld; have faith in his prophets and you will be successful." After consulting the people, Jehoshaphat **appointed men to sing to the Lord and to praise him** for the splendor of his holiness as they went out at the head of the army, saying:*
>
> *"Give thanks to the Lord, for his love endures forever."*
>
> ***As they began to sing and praise**, the Lord set ambushes against the men of Ammon and Moab and Mount Seir who were invading Judah, and they were defeated.*
>
> —2 Chronicles 20:17-22

Notice how Jehoshaphat, caught in the biggest battle of his life, chose to praise God as his weapon, and it worked! He knew that, "*The weapons we fight with are not the weapons of the world. On the contrary, they have divine power to demolish strongholds*" (2 Corinthians 10:4). The king and his army sent the praise and worship leaders out front, before the army. Do you know that they praised their way to victory? The sound of their praises defeated their enemies before they ever got to the battle.

Praise is shock and awe against the devil. He can't stand it! That's why the Bible says, "*Let the high praises of God be in their throats and two-edged swords in their hands*" (Psalm 149:6, ESV).

Praise can destroy what's in your way, like it did for the children of Israel who marched around Jericho praising God. The walls crumbled before them, and they were able to take the city.

Praise makes the jailhouse rock, like it did for Paul and Silas in prison. They lifted their voices and focused their attention on the only One who could save them. It shook the place where they were, and they were set free.

Praise gets our eyes off of our problem and onto our promise.

Praise prevents costly battles, like it did for King Jehoshaphat. That's because it scares and confuses the enemy!

Praise reminds us and others how great God is.

What Is Worship?

Throughout the darkest seasons of my life, worship has been all the sweeter, because Jesus became my main sustenance. Worshipping Him has always been a breath of fresh air during seasons of stifling questions and complications, heartbreaks, or holdups.

So what is worship? The word *worship* means "first kiss," and it's our hearts' response to who God is. Anyone can praise and speak of God's mighty deeds—but it takes a revelation of *who God is* to be able to worship Him with intimacy.

Worship is born out of an intimate relationship with Him. It is loving Him with our first kiss. Worship is like breathing for our spirits. We breathe in the fragrance of Jesus, and we breathe out the toxins from this life. We can exhale stress, fear, doubt, and anger in just one moment of being in His presence. Everything changes when He's in the room! Hebrews 12:28 (ESV) says:

> *Therefore let us be grateful for receiving a kingdom that cannot be shaken, and thus let us offer to God acceptable worship, with reverence and awe.*

Our response to all the good things we have learned about God's Kingdom and His goodness is to worship Him with our whole hearts. And it's in worshipping Him that we find our greatest enjoyment and fulfillment in life. C.S. Lewis, the greatest philosopher of the twentieth century, said, "In commanding us to glorify Him, God is inviting us to enjoy Him."

One of the greatest side benefits of worshipping God is that we find our true identities. Greater than any other job description or title, we are worshippers, because only those God has invited into His house as His children can be in close relationship with Him. The fact that we can worship Him says that we are close.

For instance, as a parallel, my husband might invite an acquaintance to a restaurant for lunch. He might invite friends over to our house. But in the morning when we all first wake up, he invites our small children into our bed, where they all pile in and have a chat before the day starts. We share our secrets, our dreams, our hurts, our joys. We might have a tickle fight, or we might just snuggle. I love those sweet times of just *being* with our little kids. Not doing. Not rushing. No agendas. Just time together. And that's what Father God wants with His kids. It doesn't have to be formal. It doesn't need to be scripted, and it shouldn't be hurried. It's just *being* with Him, inviting Him into our lives throughout the day.

In the presence of the Healer and Savior, everything changes! He is where our true power and purpose and fulfillment come from. We must remain desperate for Him, hungry for His Words. He is the source of life. There is nothing else that really compares. There is no love like His, and in His love we find our voices, we find our strength, we find our song. Once you've been in the presence of Jesus, you will feel your faith soar and your burdens roll off.

Like I said in *Healed Overnight*:

> There's danger in being around religion but not maintaining a relationship with God, Himself. Some of us who have been raised in the church or in "religion" have started slipping

away from the love and passion we had for God at first. We may want something from God, but we haven't taken time to first be *in love* with Him. We have allowed ourselves to become inoculated by the world. God said in Revelation 2:4 (NLT), *"But I have this complaint against you. You don't love me or each other as you did at first!"*

Let's commit today to stay connected to THE Life Source, and He shall renew our strength. Let's fight our battles with our hands lifted, on our knees, voices ringing out in songs of praise and worship. Let's not make this complicated. It's all about getting back to a childlike state of innocence, trust, and love for our Father. That's where true victory is found.

READ

Mark 6:31, Psalm 91:1-2

DETOX:

This week, stop praising your problems. Every time you catch yourself talking about your problems, start praising God instead.

SELF-REFLECTION:

What's keeping you from spending time alone with God? If you already have that practice, is there something you could eliminate from your life that would deepen your ability to "abide" in Him? Ask the Holy Spirit to show you ways in which you can draw even closer to God and be in His presence more and more often.

TODAY'S TAKEAWAY:

I will praise and worship Jesus through this season, because He is my very breath.

PRAYER

Jesus, take me to that secret place where we can just be. I want You more than I want anything else in this world. Take me closer to Your heart, in love with all You are. Thank You that as I spend time with You, I become more like You and do the things that You did to help people.

TESTIMONY:

"I am writing to you to testify of such a wonderful miracle I experienced from the Lord. I had called in for prayer last year regarding a serious health situation from a kidney stone. I had watched an episode on healing that shared Amy Keesee Freudiger's miraculous testimony. It spoke to me because I was in her situation. I purchased the healing set with her book, and it truly helped me to receive.

"You see, I had an X-ray done that showed I had a kidney stone that was at least 4-6mm in size and was stuck in my ureter with hydronephrosis, which was swelling of my kidney. Another diagnosis doctors said I was born with was "malrotation," when the intestines are slightly twisted and positioned on the opposite side of the colon. My husband and I immediately went into prayer since we now had something to pinpoint our prayers against. I had to see a urologist, and the doctor tried to pressure me to do surgery ASAP. He said he had very little hope. He gave me a 5% chance for the stone to pass and expressed fear of me losing my kidney if I did not go through with surgery. I told him I needed to go home and discuss this further with my husband before making any decision for surgery.

"New Year's morning 2017, I was somewhere between sleeping and waking when I felt a presence moving up and down over my left side. When I took off my clothing for a shower, there was that kidney stone in my underwear! I was stunned to say the least! My husband flipped out! He could not believe it! This was nothing short of a miracle! God is glorious! Jesus is amazing! No surgery needed!"

—E.M.

PRAISE HIM FOR VICTORY

JUST KEEP STANDING

DAY 30

To boxers face each other in the ring. As they start throwing punches at one another, they have one objective in mind: knock the other person to the mat. They both know that if one of them gets knocked out, it's all over. In sumo wrestling, the goal is much the same: get your opponent to the ground. If they can't keep standing, you win.

You've come this far in your 30-day Healing Dare. People often ask me what to do at this point, after they have learned who they are in Christ, repainted their picture of possibility, built their faith muscles, prayed the prayer of agreement, and praised God for the victory. The answer is to keep doing what you've been doing. *Keep standing.*

There comes a moment when you've done all you can do, and now you have one thing left to do—just stand. It is through faith and patience that a farmer gets the bumper crop for which he sowed. It is through faith and patience that we inherit the promises of God.

When the children of Israel were caught between the Red Sea and Pharaoh's army—a foe that had kept them enslaved for 400 years and from whom they had finally escaped—they were tempted to panic. They didn't want to go back to slavery. Yet the circumstances looked impossible. There they were, with no weapons and no training for battle, facing the armed forces of the mightiest empire on Earth at the time. But faith rose up in Moses:

> *Moses answered the people, "Do not be afraid. Stand firm and you will see the deliverance the Lord will bring you today. The Egyptians you see today you will never see again."*
> —Exodus 14:13

God spoke through Moses to His people and said that if they would simply stand in faith—not fear—then the problem facing them would never be seen again. Sure enough, they stood their ground, and God split the Red Sea in front of them. They crossed over on dry ground. But what happened next was even more astounding: God used the Red Sea—the very obstacle that stood in their way—to DROWN THEIR ENEMY. The sea crashed over the Egyptian army and drowned every last one of them, never to be seen again.

God will use the very obstacle that stood in your way to drown your enemy! The very process of standing causes you to grow and get stronger. One of these days, you will take up that object used against you, and you will do some serious damage to the kingdom of darkness.

You will share your testimony with many.

You will see others learn from what you have walked through.

When you get strong in an area that used to be an issue, you can use that strength to deliver others.

The very areas I used to struggle with have become my strength, and I minister to others in those very areas. Isn't that just like the goodness of God to turn it around?!

> *Therefore put on the full armor of God, so that when the day of evil comes, you may be able to stand your ground, and <u>after you have done everything to stand. Stand firm then</u>.*
> —Ephesians 6:13-14a

In other words, you have prepared yourself for this stand.

You pulled yourself out of your doubt and self-pity, up to a standing position.

You have marked your line in the sand and said enough is enough.

You have built your faith muscles.

You have prepared your mind and heart for battle.

You have opened your eyes to the Truth.

You are ready for this. You are ready for this stand.

Now do it! Stand firm and don't back down. Don't let any measly, sniveling demon from hell talk you out of your inheritance. Don't let the deceiver speak. Stand your ground.

Join the Faith Hall of Fame

Your weakness is the very thing that you can become strong in. Hebrews 11 is the Faith Hall of Fame in the Bible. It talks about all of the people in the Bible who didn't think they could do it, who faced impossible circumstances, who looked like they were going under, and yet they stood, and God helped them do the impossible.

Speaking about those people of faith:

>   *...who through faith conquered kingdoms, administered jus-*

tice, and gained what was promised; who shut the mouths of lions, quenched the fury of the flames, and escaped the edge of the sword; <u>whose weakness was turned to strength; and who became powerful in battle</u> and routed foreign armies. Women received back their dead, raised to life again.

—Hebrews 11:33-35a

Whatever it is that you have been pressing toward, DO NOT QUIT. You are called into the fight not to lose but to win. Hebrews 10:35-39 say:

<u>So do not throw away your confidence</u>; it will be richly rewarded. You need to persevere so that when you have done the will of God, <u>you will receive what he has promised</u>. For,

"In just a little while, he who is coming will come and will not delay."

And, "But my righteous one will live by faith. And I take no pleasure in the one who shrinks back."

But <u>we do not belong to those who shrink back and are destroyed, but to those who have faith and are saved</u>.

God doesn't want us to be destroyed by the world's problems or the enemy's schemes, so He commands us to stand and have faith. Through that stand, we wear the enemy out— and through our faith, we give God legal access to move on our behalves. By choice of our free will, we are believing in God's power to save and giving Him legal access to move.

He won't violate our free will to choose what we believe. He won't violate our hearts' convictions. But when we give Him permission in our hearts to move, through our unshakable faith in Him, He can change time, matter, nature, and direction. There's nothing beyond His scope of ability. *But it starts with us.*

We might feel afraid on the inside, but if we won't let that fear steer our words, decisions, or actions, we will see victory in every area of our lives. Emotions will arise to contradict the promise of God, and that's normal.

Emotions are just reactions to stimuli. Just tell your emotions to be quiet, and then put the right picture in front of your eyes and in your ears.

Thoughts will arise that contradict God's promise, and that's okay, but grab them and throw them out by speaking the Truth. As the saying goes, we might not be able to control what birds fly over our heads, but we can keep them from building nests in our hair.

As you close out this 30-day Healing Dare, remind yourself not to give up, grow weary, or get discouraged. Isaiah 50:7 says, "*Because the Sovereign Lord helps me, I will not be disgraced. Therefore have I set my face like flint, and I know I will not be put to shame.*" So when the devil tries to get in your face, put on your poker face and speak the Word. Just keep standing. Greater is He that is in you than he that is in the world (1 John 4:4).

Congratulations on completing your own 30-day Healing Dare! This isn't the end; it is just the beginning. Please read the following chapter, called "Next Steps," for further faith-building encouragement.

 **READ**

Jeremiah 6:16, Matthew 7:24-29

 DETOX:

As you build your life upon the rock of God's Word, build your faith, and stand against the tricks of the devil, think about ways to shore up the ground you have already taken in these past 30 days. How can you occupy this new territory, so to speak? How can you keep yourself in a place of peace and faith? What things in the atmosphere of your life need to change permanently in order to retain your victory?

 SELF-REFLECTION:

Look how far you've come! Think of all the Scripture you have hidden in your heart! I'm so proud of all you have accomplished during this dare, and I challenge you to continue walking in freedom. Take a moment to write a letter of gratitude to Father God for all He has taught you recently. Praise Him for the things He will continue to do in your life. And finally, thank Him for the total manifestation of your healing—spirit, soul, and body.

TODAY'S TAKEAWAY:

In standing on the promises of God, I am getting stronger day by day. I will not be shaken or talked down off of my trust in God. I am a receiver, not a doubter.

PRAYER

God, help me to take my stand and not back down. Give me Your strength today to walk in faith instead of fear. Lord, you said that You always cause me to triumph through You. I will not allow anything to move me. I am Your child, filled with Your Spirit, and I know that You are with me always.

Conclusion

NEXT STEPS

C ongratulations, you did it! I'm so honored to have been a part of your 30-day Healing Dare, and I hope that this journey has been empowering.

Let's address a few next steps you can take and some tools you'll need for days 31 and beyond.

Dealing with Doubt

It's hard to argue with the Word of God and with the fruit it brings. Once you experience the promises for yourself, it's a whole new level!

But what happens if you haven't experienced the fruit, or the promises, yet?

You have to fight doubt. And one of the best ways to stay encouraged is to take in other people's testimonies of victories.

Listen, I've seen many, many people healed. I was healed. I have seen people raised from the dead. I have seen the power of God transform a person's life and nature.

There are so many healing testimonies out there online and in other amazing books.

One of my favorites is *Healed of Cancer* by Dodie Osteen.

There's also a whole section of video testimonies on our church's website, FaithLifeChurch.org. There are many blogs and YouTube videos out there telling of miraculous healings by the power of God. Seek out those testimonies to help you stay encouraged and in faith.

Also, take your regimen of Daily Faith Boosters as if your life depends on it. Even *after* you receive your healing fully manifested in your body, DON'T STOP.

Just like you can't stop drinking water and expect to stay hydrated, you can't live off of yesterday's faith. Just living in this fallen world takes faith, and it's easy to become contaminated by fear since it's all around us. We must stay in faith by living and breathing the Word of God.

Speak against doubt-filled thoughts, and don't allow them back in. Like I said before, don't let satan finish his sentence. Speak the Word of God continuously over your situation, and declare the victory that was ALREADY paid for.

The profound magnitude of what Jesus did for each one of us cannot be expressed in words, and I know that none of us will truly understand or appreciate it until we get on the other side of this life. But we can certainly start celebrating it to the best of our understanding right here and now! I never want to lose the joy of salvation in all of its purity, innocence, and simplicity. That joy will strengthen and sustain us.

If you're still having doubts or more questions about a specific theological (man-made) objection to supernatural healing, check out the chapter "Top Questions About Healing" from my book *Healed Overnight: Five Steps to Accessing Supernatural Healing*.

The Power of the Holy Spirit

Just before Jesus left the earth, He told the disciples about a gift He would leave them, and that gift was the Holy Spirit. Acts 1:4-8 talk about Jesus's promise:

> *On one occasion, while he was eating with them, he gave them this command: "Do not leave Jerusalem, but wait for the gift my Father promised, which you have heard me speak about. For John baptized with water, but in a few days you will be baptized with the Holy Spirit."*
>
> *Then they gathered around him and asked him, "Lord, are you at this time going to restore the kingdom to Israel?"*
>
> *He said to them: "It is not for you to know the times or dates the Father has set by his own authority. **But you will receive power when the Holy Spirit comes on you; and you will be my witnesses** in Jerusalem, and in all Judea and Samaria, and to the ends of the earth."*

So Jesus was talking about a new power the disciples would receive after He had ascended to heaven. That power would come as the result of the Holy Spirit dwelling in us and baptizing us with His anointing and ability.

In Acts 2:32-33, the disciples had just received this gift on what is now called The Day of Pentecost, and Peter stands up to preach under this amazing new power. He says,

> *"God has raised this Jesus to life, and we are all witnesses of it.*

Exalted to the right hand of God, he has received from the Father **_the promised Holy Spirit_** *and has poured out what you now see and hear."*

Peter and the other disciples went on to do all the works that Jesus did, healing the sick, raising the dead, and preaching with power. They showed us what a life looks like under the influence of God's anointing.

So the Holy Spirit is in us when we are born again into God's Kingdom, and He is there to guide, strengthen, and comfort us. He is the power we need to live this life. However, there's a difference between having the Holy Spirit in our lives and actually operating under His power.

When we are baptized in the Holy Spirit, as is mentioned in the first chapter of Acts, we are filled with power to do the works that Jesus did. We receive the *anointing* of the Holy Spirit when we are baptized by Him. It's a baptism of POWER.

All you have to do to receive the baptism in the Holy Spirit is to welcome Him. He will come.

The baptism in the Holy Spirit is a free gift given to every believer as empowerment to live this life with authority, wisdom, counsel, and strength.

You can learn more about this incredible gift by checking out the book *The Baptism in the Holy Spirit* by Gary Keesee.

Freedom in Every Way

Sometimes, people face turmoil or mental torment, such as feeling confused, angry, afraid, depressed, or unable to sleep. Sometimes they have really bad dreams or bad things happening all the time for no apparent reason. Perhaps it's gone on for years with no relief. Have you experienced anything like that? If it continues and isn't just a bad day, consider that it might be a demonic spirit trying to oppress you. Now, there's absolutely no need to fear! It's simply something that needs dealt with spiritually. Once you recognize it and call it out, it must go. You have authority!

However, we often don't even realize what's going on, but we know we aren't ourselves and don't know why. We sometimes can't see the attack from our perspective. There are demonic spirits that want to try and toy with Christians' emotions, but they want to stay hidden because they know they have to go if called out. *They can only stay if they are given a right to stay.* Demonic spirits look for weak spots in people's lives, such as sin, addiction, unbelief, fear, or occult involvement. They use that as an entrance into that person's life. Any sin that has not been surrendered under the blood of Jesus can be a legal entrance into that person's life. This especially includes previous involvement in witchcraft, occultism, or other evil practices.

I have noticed a trend in some people I've prayed for who have unexplained illnesses or pain, and that is that sometimes there was an open door to witchcraft in their past. If they had any part in occultism, spiritism, New Age practices, or witchcraft (using Ouija boards, attending séances, playing the game *Dungeons and Dragons*, dabbling in practices that are not of God, etc.), there can remain an opening for the devil to continue to torment them. This can only happen when a Christian does not repent of that activity and allows that spirit to stay, perhaps unknowingly.

One day, my friend and I did a prayer session with a lady who had little time left to live, or so the doctors had told her. She had a wide-eyed look, and her eyes were pools of deep sadness. After hearing her list of ailments (and there were many), I started praying in the Holy Spirit. The Lord gave me a picture in my mind of her as a little girl sitting in the middle of a pentagram painted on a hardwood floor. I saw that she had been used in occult rituals from a young age. When I asked her if that was the case, she was shocked and confirmed that her mother had been a witch and she had indeed been used for those purposes. Her mother had actually dedicated her to the devil as the "devil's child" when she was just a tiny girl. How horrid!

I explained to her that as a Christian, she did not have to live in fear of demonic powers. She did not have to allow those spirits of witchcraft to torment her any longer. She needed to break that oath her mother had spoken over her life. The sad thing was, she had no idea that she had authority over those demonic presences! She knew they were there but had no idea how to deal with them. That day, she trusted Jesus for freedom, and we prayed. I had her rebuke those demonic spirits and forbid their presence in her life. After crying tears of release and healing for some time, she physically relaxed, and she looked up at me with clear eyes. They actually sparkled with joy by the time she left there, and she was so happy, light, and at peace. She also reported later that the physical pain she had suffered was going away day by day.

Having also been tormented by a spirit of infirmity for many years, I recognize it in others now. It has to go! It has no right to remain! It's a legal issue, not a "feeling" issue. Legally, you are God's property, so they must stop trespassing!

Jesus didn't allow demonic spirits to stay in people's lives. He operated in "deliverance ministry" and cast out demons wherever He went. He treated many illnesses as a deliverance issue, not a physical issue. One day, when a crippled lady asked for healing, He said to the Pharisees watching his every move:

> *"Then should not this woman, a daughter of Abraham, whom Satan has kept bound for eighteen long years, **be set free** on the Sabbath day from what bound her?"*
> —Luke 13:16

He prayed for her, and she was instantly healed. She was free! You, too, can be set free from turmoil, infirmity, or whatever has you feeling constrained and held down. Where the Spirit of the Lord is, there is freedom and liberty (2 Corinthians 3:17). Take your stand against those harassments, and receive the freedom of Jesus in your life.

Be aware that the lying spirits you have been freed from over the past 30 days (such as spirits of rejection, self-hatred, fear, or infirmity) might try to come back and see if you will let them back in. How do you let them back in? By coming into agreement with the thoughts they try to give you. Jesus said that once a spirit leaves, it will come back to see if you are guarding the door to the house or if there is a way back in (Luke 11:21-28). The door represents your mind, and your house represents your heart. That's why the Bible says, *"Above all else, guard your heart, for everything you do flows from it"* (Proverbs

4:23). Be listening and looking for signs that you are falling for a lie again. Stand guard at the door to your thoughts and to your heart.

Don't allow messages of fear back in. If you recognize where those bad thoughts are coming from, stand strong, and command them to go. Be very self-aware, and call out those intruders before they can break into your heart (your house). Leif Hetland says that there is a battle you fight after the battle you win. It's the battle to remain in faith and stand guard against the return of that familiar spirit in your life.

Keep your armor on! Continue to stand! Be on your guard against those voices and thoughts that would try to derail your faith. Immediately interrupt them and forbid them from coming back. Command them to go the moment you sense something is not right.

Again, it's in the standing that you get stronger and more powerful. You have no need to fear, because they all must bow to the name of Jesus and the authority that you carry through Him.

If you aren't sure what could be the root problem when you feel oppressed or down, I recommend receiving prayer from someone who understands the spiritual world and their authority in Christ. We sometimes cannot see what we are up against because it feels so familiar to us. This kind of prayer is sometimes called a prayer of deliverance, but it simply means that someone with the gift of discernment prays over you and helps you to discern what is going on so that you can stand against it together. Understand that the prayer of deliverance is not a prerequisite for receiving healing, but demonic activity *might be* the root cause of illness. And even after being physically healed, there still might be some of that past junk hanging around that needs to be dealt with. The prayer of agreement with someone who understands the spiritual realm and operates in the gift of discernment is so powerful in calling those things out. It's by the Holy Spirit any of us can understand what is happening, but sometimes we need a partner in the fight.

For continued resources on this topic of freedom, there is an awesome book and small group study by Pastor Chris Hodges called *Living in Freedom Every Day*, and many churches in the USA host these groups. I have been through this small group study several times, and each time, there has been such freedom that comes into my life as a result.

Let Me Pray for You

Prayer is a powerful weapon against the enemy, and words filled with faith accomplish so much!

As I write this, I join my faith with yours, and I speak life to your body and health to your bones. I come against this spirit of infirmity attacking your body and your family. I say that it MUST bow its knee to the authority inside of you. You are God's child, and no demonic spirit has ANY power over you or your family, in Jesus's name.

I pray that you know how much Jesus loves you and that you accept a full restoration of your identity as His child. You know who you are in Christ, and you will not listen to any lies of shame, discouragement, or insecurity, in the name of Jesus.

I speak against pain, and I say to pain, "You get out now, in the name of Jesus! You are trespassing against God's child. You are no longer permitted here!"

Friend, I declare that you are making a full recovery to live your best life. This will be your healthiest year yet! You will live and not die and will declare the works of the Lord. Greater things lie ahead than what lies behind. I pray that you know your authority in Christ and that you fill your heart with God's Word.

I pray that as you walk in this, your joy will overflow, your life will shine forth God's praises, and you will begin to minister it to others. I believe with you that your life will be a witness to so many, and your testimony of healing will change lives, in Jesus's name.

It's Your Time to Thrive

As we conclude this devotional, I encourage you to step out boldly in all that you have learned. Don't stop doing the things you have put into practice! It changed my life, and I know it will change yours. You have planted the seeds, but do not stop watering and nourishing those seeds. You are going to reap the rewards if you don't quit. (See Galatians 6:9.)

Over the past 30 days, we have studied five key areas that will bring victory to every area of your life, including to your health. It was during my own 30-day Healing Dare that these five steps were revealed to me with clarity.

While God had tried to get those things across to me before then, they didn't click until those 30 days. I had grown up in church hearing some of those concepts, but they weren't personal to me until then. During my Dare, they became revelation instead of head knowledge. I trust that you, too, have had the Word come to life in your spirit over these past 30 days.

Remember the Five Keys

IDENTITY is the foundation. Who you are in Christ affects what you can receive. You are a child of God, a co-heir with Christ to all the promises of God. When you reclaim your lost identity, you know your Father's heart for you, and you can be confident in your place at His table.

FAITH paints the picture of possibility. Faith sees the after picture when you are still living in the before. Faith is agreement with God! As you sow the Word of God into your life, it produces faith in your heart all by itself until one day, your picture has changed on the inside to match heaven's picture for your life.

AUTHORITY is the power to enforce the victory. Remember, the victory was already paid for and given to you by Jesus. You live in a finished work, in a New Covenant. However, you must stand in your authority against the devil's lies and use your given authority to decree things on Earth and actively be a doer of the Word. You must not back down!

AGREEMENT is the petition spoken in faith. Once you are in faith, fully persuaded of God's promise for you, it's time to pray the prayer of agreement, during which you release the power of the Holy

Spirit to enforce the victory. This is your "so be it" in response to God's "I will." When you speak God's Word in faith, it will accomplish what it was sent to do.

PRAISE is the posture you take once you have prayed. After you mark that place of receiving by faith, the moment you pray becomes your line in the sand. It is your "it is finished" moment. Now it's time to thank God for the victory! It's time to praise Him. During this season of standing, your body is recovering, you are receiving strength, and you are being renewed, even if you don't see it on the outside. It's a season of standing on the promises. Turn up some music from our group, Open Heaven Band, and remind yourself of the great God you serve! (We write faith-building songs filled with God's Word! No Christian fatalism here!)

The Best Is Yet to Come

What an incredible journey this has been, and I want to encourage you that this is just the tip of the iceberg, the very beginning of a brand-new season. It was for me!

Once I received my healing, I can honestly say it was the beginning of the best season of my life. There was a time of tearful rejoicing, months of reflecting on what I learned, opportunities to tell others what had happened, the joy of seeing other's lives changed as a result, and many days of celebrating the impact of my healing in so many areas.

I got pregnant with my first child one year later. We have since had three beautiful children, and I love being a mom! My husband and

I have traveled the globe, both for leisure and to share my story. We have walked out these five steps in other areas of life and have seen incredible fruit. The same principles apply!

Be sure to check out the appendix of this book, where you will find my favorite healing Scriptures and my declaration of faith that I spoke over myself when I was sick.

Also, check out my website HealedOvernight.com for more books, teaching resources, worship music, blogs, and testimonies. I highly recommend you read the companion book to this devotional, called, *Healed Overnight: Five Steps to Accessing Supernatural Healing*.

I would also LOVE to hear from you! Please let me know how this 30-day Healing Dare has impacted you! You can contact me at healedovernight.com, on YouTube (Amy Freudiger), Instagram @amyfreudiger, or Facebook.com/amykeeseefreudiger.

I'm excited to say this is the beginning of your BEST years. The greatest victories lie ahead. The deeper understanding and richer relationship with Jesus that you have gained and continue to gain will impact every area. The time you have invested into this will not return void. It will bring a harvest of health, restoration, abundance, and joy into your life, in Jesus's name.

 **READ**

Daniel 6:26-27

 **DETOX:**

What have you been freed from and are walking away from forever?

 SELF-REFLECTION:

What has changed on the inside of you since you started this 30-day Healing Dare? What has changed on the outside?

 TAKEAWAY:

Stay in the fight, and keep on this journey. Stand tall, "*being confident of this, that he who began a good work in you will carry it on to completion until the day of Christ Jesus*" (Philippians 1:6).

PRAYER

Thank you, Lord, that, since Your Spirit that raised Jesus from the dead is living in me, You will also give life to my mortal body because of Your Spirit who lives in me. Lord, I thank You that Your resurrection power is changing and reviving every part of my life. It is renewing my strength. It is restoring my vitality. All the dead dreams are coming back to life, in Jesus's name.

Appendix

HEALING SCRIPTURES

YOUR DAILY DOSE OF TRUTH

T hese are Scriptures to speak out loud every day, hopefully SEVERAL times per day, during your 30-day Healing Dare! This is your Truth Medicine, and you must take it like a good patient.

I know you will see it start to radically transform your mind and body. God's Word is living and active—not like regular words. They are Spirit words, breathed and spoken by the Life Giver, Himself. When you speak them using your own voice, your body reacts and goes into action to enact these Truths.

I encourage you to keep them with you constantly, speak them several times per day, and insert your own name to personalize each one where appropriate. These are the promises of God!

Meditate on the Word of God constantly, as if it is your very breath. Speak it out loud. Think about it all day. Let it roll around in your mind and spirit.

The Word of God is made of spirit, just like your body is made of cells. When you speak the healing Word, you are literally rebuilding your body in the spirit realm, cell by cell. Soon it will be visible in the natural realm!

Healing Scriptures:

Surely he took up our pain and bore our suffering, yet we considered him punished by God, stricken by him, and afflicted. But he was pierced for our transgressions, he was crushed for our iniquities; the punishment that brought us peace was on him, and by his wounds we are healed.

—Isaiah 53:4-5

But if the Spirit of him that raised up Jesus from the dead dwell in you, he that raised up Christ from the dead shall also quicken your mortal bodies by his Spirit that dwelleth in you.

—Romans 8:11 (KJV)

They shall lay hands on the sick, and they shall recover.

—Mark 16:18b (KJV)

God is not human, that he should lie, not a human being, that he should change his mind. Does he speak and then not act? Does he promise and not fulfill?

—Numbers 23:19

Every good and perfect gift is from above, coming down from the Father of the heavenly lights, who does not change like shifting shadows.

—James 1:17

I have given you authority to trample on snakes and scorpions and to overcome all the power of the enemy; nothing will harm you.

—Luke 10:19

Praise the Lord, my soul, and forget not all his benefits—who forgives all your sins and heals all your diseases.

—Psalm 103:2-3

Dear friend, I pray that you may enjoy good health and that all may go well with you, even as your soul is getting along well.

—3 John 1:2

He will take our weak mortal bodies and change them into glorious bodies like his own, using the same power with which he will bring everything under his control.

—Philippians 3:21 (NLT)

Is anyone among you sick? Then he must call for the elders of the church and they are to pray over him, anointing him with oil in the name of the Lord; and the prayer of faith will restore the one who is sick, and the Lord will raise him up, and if he has committed sins, they will be forgiven him.

—James 5:14-15 (NASB)

Yet he did not waver through unbelief regarding the promise of God, but was strengthened in his faith and gave glory to God, being fully persuaded that God had power to do what he had promised.

—Romans 4:20-21 (talking about Abraham)

He sent out his word and healed them; he rescued them from the grave.

—Psalm 107:20

When Jesus came into Peter's house, he saw Peter's mother-in-law lying in bed with a fever. He touched her hand and the fever left her, and she got up and began to wait on him. When evening came, many who were demon-possessed were brought to him, and he drove out the spirits with a word and healed all the sick. This was to fulfill what was spoken through the prophet Isaiah: "He took up our infirmities and bore our diseases."

—Matthew 8:14-17

They will have no fear of bad news; their hearts are steadfast, trusting in the Lord.

—Psalm 112:7

Lord my God, I called to you for help and you healed me.

—Psalm 30:2

Jesus turned and saw her. "Take heart, daughter," he said, "your faith has healed you." And the woman was healed from that moment.

—Matthew 9:22

Heal me, Lord, and I will be healed; save me and I will be saved, for you are the one I praise.

—Jeremiah 17:14

And you know that God anointed Jesus of Nazareth with the Holy Spirit and with power. Then Jesus went around doing good and healing all who were oppressed by the devil, for God was with him.

—Acts 10:38 (NLT)

Let God be true, and every human being a liar.

—Romans 3:4a

Now faith is the substance of things hoped for, the evidence of things not seen.

—Hebrews 11:1 (KJV)

For no matter how many promises God has made, they are "Yes" in Christ. And so through him the "Amen" is spoken by us to the glory of God.

—2 Corinthians 1:20

The thief comes only to steal and kill and destroy; I have come that they may have life, and have it to the full.

—John 10:10

Or do you not know that your body is a temple of the Holy Spirit who is in you, whom you have from God, and that you are not your own? For you were bought with a price: therefore glorify God in your body.

—1 Corinthians 6:19-20 (NKJV)

Therefore I say unto you, What things soever ye desire, when ye pray, believe that ye receive them, and ye shall have them.

—Mark 11:24 (KJV)

But for you who fear my name, the Sun of Righteousness will rise with healing in his wings. And you will go free, leaping with joy like calves let out to pasture.

—Malachi 4:2 (NLT)

So they set out and went from village to village, proclaiming the good news and healing people everywhere.

—Luke 9:6

...who had come to hear him and to be healed of their diseases. Those troubled by impure spirits were cured, and the people all

tried to touch him, because power was coming from him and healing them all.

—Luke 6:18-19

God also bound himself with an oath, so that those who received the promise could be perfectly sure that he would never change his mind.

—Hebrews 6:17 (NLT)

I will exalt you, Lord, for you rescued me. You refused to let my enemies triumph over me. O Lord my God, I cried to you for help, and you restored my health. You brought me up from the grave; O Lord. You kept me from falling into the pit of death. Weeping may last through the night, but joy comes with the morning. You have turned my mourning into joyful dancing.

—Psalm 30:1-3, 5b, 11a (NLT)

You will not fear the terror of night, nor the arrow that flies by day, nor the pestilence that stalks in the darkness, nor the plague that destroys at midday. A thousand may fall at your side, ten thousand at your right hand, but it will not come near you.

—Psalm 91:5-7

Nevertheless, I will bring health and healing to it; I will heal my people and will let them enjoy abundant peace and security.

—Jeremiah 33:6

It has come at last—salvation and power and the Kingdom of our God, and the authority of his Christ. For the accuser of our brothers and sisters has been thrown down to earth—the one who accuses them before our God day and night. And they have defeated him by the blood of the Lamb and by their testimony.

—Revelation 12:10-11a (NLT)

By faith in the name of Jesus, this man whom you see and know was made strong. It is Jesus' name and the faith that comes through him that has completely healed him, as you can all see.

—Acts 3:16

| Appendix

MY DAILY

FAITH DECLARATION

T his is the confession I spoke over myself daily, after some time in worship and after I had spoken my healing Scriptures out loud.

I want you to pray over yourself daily as you believe for total health, using either this faith declaration or your own that you write.

Always base your confession on what God's Word says!

> Father, thank You that You love me, and You call me precious. I submit myself to You right now. You are my King and Sovereign. I ask You to cleanse my heart of any sin or unrighteousness. I forgive and release anyone who has harmed me. I forgive myself, and I bind condemnation. I belong to You. My best days are ahead of me!

> I praise You for Your promises to me! You said that the same resurrection power that brought Jesus out of the grave is now restoring and quickening my mortal body. I receive it now. I believe that You sent Jesus to pay the price for my healing. You said that by His wounds, I am healed. I believe Your Word is true for me today.

> I command the spirit of infirmity to leave my body now and never return! You evil spirit of sickness, I belong to God Most High, and according to the blood Jesus shed on the cross, I have authority over you. I bind you and command you to go! Every symptom must leave! Pain, be gone, in Jesus's name. I will live and not die and will declare the works of the Lord. Greater is He that is in me than anything in this world. I've

been given power to trample on the enemy, and nothing shall by any means harm me. Body, I call forth the anointing on the inside of me to flood you with life. I command you to line up with God's Truth. You are healed! God said it, and I believe it. It is finished! Amen.

Once I spoke this confession over myself, I would spend the last few minutes of my prayer time speaking to specific body parts to be normal and healed.

I would command illness, disease, tumors, or anything else violating my body to wither and die at the roots. I would curse the spirit of infirmity and command it to go. I learned that the power of life and death are in my words, and I'm convinced that every time I spoke this confession, my body was recovering! Heavy-duty lifting was being done in the spiritual realm even though I couldn't see it with my physical eyes. I know when you speak God's Word, it will do the same in your life. What He did for me in healing my body, He does for all who believe.

ABOUT THE AUTHOR

Amy Keesee Freudiger has a passion to see people encounter the presence of the Living God, just as she did when she was miraculously and instantly healed of a 13-pound tumor. Since then, Amy has been on a mission to share the Truths that she learned on her journey, and she wants to help others walk free from infirmity.

As a speaker, worship leader, author, and songwriter, her bold faith and sensitivity to God's presence have resulted in many others being healed. She has always had a heart to see generational revival and supernatural healing in families.

Amy is Worship Pastor at Faith Life Church, a diverse and multi-generational church near Columbus, Ohio. She has done everything from mop floors to lead kids' ministry, and has served since she was 11 years old. (Her parents, Gary and Drenda Keesee, are the founding pastors—all the pastor's kids said, "Amen." Haha!)

Amy is also a recording artist and songwriter with Open Heaven Band (www.openheavenband.com). From being a vocal performance major in college to performing for an audience of one in worship, music has always been a natural and important part of her life.

Amy lives in Central Ohio with her amazing husband, Jason, and their three beautiful miracles: daughter Journey (Amy's mini-me) and sons Dawson and Revere. Amy enjoys traveling, homeschooling their children, taking in beautiful things, and drinking coffee while reading a good book (if her kids will give her a moment).

RESOURCES

Website: HealedOvernight.com

YouTube: Amy Freudiger

Facebook: AmyKeeseeFreudiger

Instagram: @amyfreudiger

Music: Open Heaven Band, available on all digital platforms or at OpenHeavenBand.com

Other resources: FaithLifeNow.com

Church: Faith Life Church in Central Ohio, at FaithLifeChurch.org

THE LEGAL STUFF

This book details the author's personal experiences with and opinions about healing and health. The author is not a healthcare provider, and this book is not meant to replace the advice of your healthcare provider. The author and publisher make no representations or warranties of any kind with respect to this book or its contents. The author and publisher disclaim all such representations and warranties, including for example, warranties of merchantability and healthcare for a particular purpose. In addition, the author and publisher do not represent or warrant that the information accessible via this book is accurate, complete, or current at the time of reading.

The statements made about practices, products, or services have not been evaluated by the U.S. Food and Drug Administration. They are not intended to diagnose, treat, cure, or prevent any condition or disease. Please consult with your own physician or healthcare specialist regarding the suggestions and recommendations made in this book. Neither the author nor publisher, nor any authors, contributors, or other representatives will be liable for damages arising out of or in connection with the use of this book.

This is a comprehensive limitation of liability that applies to all damages of any kind, including (without limitation) compensatory; direct, indirect or consequential damages; loss of data, income, or profit; loss of or damage to property and claims of third parties. Before you begin any healthcare program, or change your lifestyle in any way, such as starting a fast, you should consult with your physician or another licensed healthcare practitioner to ensure that you are in good health and that the examples contained in this book will not harm you. This book provides content related to physical and/or mental health issues. As such, use of this book implies your acceptance of this disclaimer.